'Pooky Knightsmith's ... atory school staff have long feared to t... ...-harm and eating disorders to supporting sufferers, from referring them to (and working with) appropriate agencies to reintegrating them into school: all that desperately needed practical common sense and potentially life-saving advice is here. An essential handbook for schools and education professionals.'

 – Bernard Trafford, Headmaster, Royal Grammar School, Newcastle upon Tyne

'This book is a wonderful resource for schools and colleges and will help committed staff to produce an environment in which eating disorders are either prevented or are detected as early as possible. This means that the individual, her/his peers and the family are supported in a timely and effective manner which can prevent the illness taking a hold. The book is authoritative and multifaceted with lived experience, academic expertise and in-depth experience of collaborative work with teachers, tutors and key school staff. An essential handbook for all schools to improve mental health by creating a sound curriculum and a healthy environment.'

 – Prof Janet Treasure, OBE PhD FRCP FRCPsych,
 Professor of Psychiatry, King's College London

'Drawing on the voices of young people, this is a truly excellent book for teachers and anyone working in schools. It offers clear, practical advice that can easily and safely be used. It will give you the confidence to support a young person facing these issues without being an expert. I highly recommend it.'

 – Clare Stafford, Chief Executive, Charlie Waller Memorial Trust

'Eating disorders are serious illnesses that are of great public health concern, given their high prevalence and adverse health consequences. Schools are excellent settings for prevention, early identification, referral for treatment and support during and following treatment. In this book, Pooky Knightsmith provides a wealth of information for school staff concerned about eating disorders and other forms of self-harm. This comprehensive book will be an important reference to have and to use within school settings. It is crucial to utilize schools in order to decrease the public health burden of eating disorders.'

 – Dianne Neumark-Sztainer, PhD, Professor at the School of
 Public Health, University of Minnesota and author of I'm, Like,
 So Fat! Helping Your Teen Make Healthy Choices about
 Eating and Exercise in a Weight-Obsessed *World*

'When children scream for help too many adults mistake the signs of mental illness as a "behaviour issue". This book is invaluable for support professionals. It unpeels complex issues with clear, practical advice allowing you to manage vulnerable children with care and confidence.'

– Paul Dix, Lead Trainer, Pivotal Education

'This is an incredibly important book, especially given the worrying rise in the number of these disorders over recent years. Pooky Knightsmith gives her readers an insight into all aspects of self-harm and eating disorders, from understanding what these disorders are, right through to supporting students and their families in overcoming them. This is a thoroughly practical and useful book that will support, advise and enlighten you and your staff. The book is given even deeper impact through the use of case studies and the real voices of young people. It is a must read for all those who work in education.'

– Sue Cowley, author, presenter and teacher trainer

'This book is a superb blend of subtle, intelligent and deeply sensible advice on eating disorders and self-harm. The combination of simple strategies and practical tips, grounded in best evidence and a wealth of up-to-date information, make it essential reading for anyone with pastoral responsibility in schools.'

– Jessica Streeting, School Nurse, Practice Teacher, Queen's Nurse

'This is a quite excellent book in that it fills a gap: giving school staff both an insight into, and an effective help "manual" for responding to eating disorders and self-destructive behaviour in young people. Like the best books it also leaves one hungry for more.'

– Dr Alan Cooklin, FRCPsych, Consultant in Family
Psychiatry, Camden and Islington NHS Foundation Trust and
Honorary Senior Lecturer, University College London

'*Self-Harm and Eating Disorders in Schools* is a comprehensive and practical guide. Pooky's clear step-by-step advice for recognising warning signs and supporting students at risk is an invaluable resource for providing teachers with the tools for empathetic and confident action. This book is a must for all upper primary and secondary teachers.'

– Cate Sangster, health and physical education teacher and author
of Ed says U Said: Eating Disorder Translator

SELF-HARM AND EATING DISORDERS IN SCHOOLS

of related interest

A Short Introduction to Understanding and Supporting Children and Young People Who Self-Harm
Carol Fitzpatrick
ISBN 978 1 84905 281 8
eISBN 978 0 85700 584 7
Part of the JKP Short Introductions series

By Their Own Young Hand
Deliberate Self-harm and Suicidal Ideas in Adolescents
Keith Hawton and Karen Rodham with Emma Evans
ISBN 978 1 84310 230 4
eISBN 978 1 84642 529 5

Ed says U said
Eating Disorder Translator
June Alexander and Cate Sangster
Foreword by Laura Collins
ISBN 978 1 84905 331 0
eISBN 978 0 85700 677 6

Maintaining Recovery from Eating Disorders
Avoiding Relapse and Recovering Life
Naomi Feigenbaum
Foreword by Rebekah Bardwell Doweyko
ISBN 978 1 84905 815 5
eISBN 978 0 85700 250 1

Essential Listening Skills for Busy School Staff
What to Say When You Don't Know What to Say
Nick Luxmoore
ISBN 978 1 84905 565 9
eISBN 978 1 78450 000 9

That's So Gay!
Challenging Homophobic Bullying
Jonathan Charlesworth
ISBN 978 1 84905 461 4
eISBN 978 0 85700 837 4

Teen Anxiety
A CBT and ACT Activity Resource Book for Helping Anxious Adolescents
Raychelle Cassada Lohmann
ISBN 978 1 84905 969 5
eISBN 978 0 85700 859 6

SELF-HARM AND EATING DISORDERS IN SCHOOLS

A Guide to Whole-School Strategies and Practical Support

POOKY KNIGHTSMITH

FOREWORD BY SARAH BRENNAN

Jessica Kingsley *Publishers*
London and Philadelphia

First published in 2015
by Jessica Kingsley Publishers
73 Collier Street
London N1 9BE, UK
and
400 Market Street, Suite 400
Philadelphia, PA 19106, USA

www.jkp.com

Library of Congress Cataloging in Publication Data
A CIP catalog record for this book is available from the Library of Congress

British Library Cataloguing in Publication Data
A CIP catalogue record for this book is available from the British Library

ISBN 978 1 84905 584 0
eISBN 978 1 78450 031 3

Printed and bound in Great Britain

*For Terry Knight, the world's best
grandfather and mentor, with thanks*

Contents

Foreword by Sarah Brennan   11

ACKNOWLEDGEMENTS   13

PREFACE   15

1. Introduction to Eating Disorders and Self-Harm   17

2. Overcoming Stigma and Exploring Common Misconceptions   30

3. Teaching Students about Self-Harm and Eating Disorders   41

4. Why Students Develop Unhealthy Coping Mechanisms   53

5. Factors that Put Students at Risk of Eating Disorders and Self-Harm   66

6. Early Symptoms of Eating Disorders and Self-Harm   78

7. Talking to Students Causing Concern   84

8. Responding to Disclosures and Self-Harm Incidents   98

9. Working with Parents   113

10. When and How to Refer a Student for Specialized Support   127

11. Supporting Students Who Require Inpatient Care   136

12. Day-to-Day Strategies for Supporting Recovery at School   144

13. The Impact of the Internet   171

14. Providing One-to-One Support   183

15. Motivational Interviewing as a Tool for Behaviour Change   207

16. The Road to Recovery   215

Index   220

Foreword

For the first time, here we have a straight-talking, easy-to-understand guide for anyone working or living with children and young people to understand mental health conditions. Professionals and families outside of the Child and Adolescent Mental Health field have for too long felt unskilled, unconfident and ignorant of basic facts about some of the most common emotional and mental health problems young people experience. There is a taboo about self-harm and eating disorders – YoungMinds found that even GPs find self-harm the most difficult subject to broach with teenagers.

So, this book is breaking new ground. Pooky has successfully drawn together a combination of technical and comprehensive information, which is described in such a way that all of us can understand and relate to it. I have no doubt that all staff in schools will find this book illuminating, but I believe a much broader audience will find it very helpful too.

This is a book that will be returned to many times by its readers, for reference, out of interest or for practical help – and it will continue to be of help to all of us.

Sarah Brennan
Chief Executive, YoungMinds

Acknowledgements

Acknowledgement of funding

This book draws on independent research commissioned by the National Institute for Health Research (NIHR) under its Programme Grants for Applied Research scheme (RP-PG-0606-1043). The views expressed in this publication are those of the author and not necessarily those of the NHS, the NIHR or the Department of Health.

Personal acknowledgements

This book is based largely on research I carried out whilst completing my PhD at the Institute of Psychiatry, King's College London. As such I would like to thank my supervisors, Professors Ulrike Schmidt and Janet Treasure, for their sizeable input into this work. I would also like to thank the many students and staff who have been brave enough and kind enough to share their experiences of self-harm and eating disorders with me during the course of my research over the past seven years. You will find them quoted throughout this book.

A huge thank you also needs to be extended to the many colleagues who viewed early drafts of this book and offered constructive feedback, innovative suggestions and words of encouragement when they were most needed. Particular thanks go to:

- Becci Hayward, Counsellor, The Guildford Institute

- Claire Corfield, Assistant Headteacher, Ysgol Bryn Alyn secondary school, Wrexham

- Cathy Wright, Head of Key Stage 3, New College Worcester

- Gill Richards, Senior Counsellor, Wiltshire College

- Jennifer Beer, Public Health Practitioner, Buckinghamshire County Council

- Jo Finnett, Maths Teacher, North Halifax Grammar School

- Joe Hayman, CEO, PSHE Association

- Laura, Youth Worker

- Laura Sturdee, Deputy Housemistress, Cranleigh School, Surrey

- Nick Bolton, Personal Development Education Adviser, Wiltshire Council

- Paula Spencer, School Counsellor, Greig City Academy, Haringey

- Rachel Monahan, Form Tutor, Latymer Upper School

- Sam Beal, Partnership Adviser: Health and Wellbeing, Brighton & Hove City Council

- Shirley Shears, Senior Tutor, Clitheroe Royal Grammar School

- Siobain Chase, Inclusion Manager, Ferndale Community Primary School, Swindon.

Thank you also to my colleagues at the PSHE Association who have taught me a huge amount and provided a great forum for exploring new ideas.

Finally, thank you to my daughters Lyra and Ellie who fill me with pride and inspiration each and every day, and to my husband Tom whose unwavering support and sense of fun ensures that I continue to teach others about supporting self-harm and eating disorders without ever feeling the need to revisit these unhelpful behaviours myself.

Preface

This book is designed as a practical guide for anyone working within a school or a similar setting who wants to improve their knowledge, skills and confidence in supporting young people suffering from self-harm or eating disorders. It is drawn largely from research conducted during the course of my PhD and many training sessions and workshops I have run on this topic for school staff, parents and students.

It does not take the place of face-to-face training, but the reality is that such training can be hard to access as there are very few people specializing in this field – I would urge you to attend training where it is possible and, where it is not, I would suggest that you explore the ideas shared within this book with your colleagues. Please treat this book as a starting point and springboard rather than a definitive set of answers.

I am UK-based, so whilst I have made every effort to make the content suitable for an international audience, care will need to be taken when adapting the ideas herein for your school or college if you work outside the UK. Parents are referred to throughout – this should be taken to mean the person who provides care to a child. The words 'student' and 'child' are also used throughout as these are words that I felt would most resonate with an international audience. Much of the content of this book can be adapted to suit working with a range of ages, from very young children right through to college-aged students and beyond. Finally, I refer several times to Child and Adolescent Mental Health Services (CAMHS); if this is not a term that is applicable to your setting, please take it to mean an external agency that is able to provide support and care to children suffering with mental health and emotional wellbeing issues.

If you require further support, you will find a wide range of free resources on my website (www.inourhands.com), including some resources designed to directly complement the contents of this book. Up-to-date lists of further sources of support are also included on my website. These change so rapidly that including them in print seemed likely to prove unhelpful.

I welcome your feedback on the contents of this book and am always more than happy to be contacted should you wish to share ideas or seek advice. I also always welcome the opportunity to share good practice through the delivery of presentations, training sessions or workshops on the topics touched upon in this book as well as related topics.

Dr Pooky Knightsmith
www.inourhands.com
pooky@inourhands.com
@PookyH

CHAPTER 1

Introduction to Eating Disorders and Self-Harm

This chapter will enable you to:

- define the three major eating disorders: anorexia nervosa, bulimia nervosa and binge eating disorder
- understand the range of eating difficulties commonly seen in children under 11
- define self-harm and learn about the most common types
- differentiate between self-harming behaviours and behaviours with suicidal intent.

Eating disorders explained

There are three major types of eating disorder: anorexia nervosa, bulimia nervosa and binge eating disorder. We'll go on to explore each of these in more depth later in the chapter. What all three of these eating disorders have in common is that the sufferer is using their food intake, their weight or their shape as a way of coping with their life day to day. On the outside, eating disorders look very different: some sufferers become so emaciated that they are prescribed complete bed rest, others become so morbidly obese that they are unable to leave their homes, but weight loss, gain or fluctuation is simply an eating disorder symptom. The thoughts, feelings and psychological makeup which accompany the different eating disorders are very similar.

Over the next few pages I've outlined the typical symptoms and characteristics we might expect to see in young people with anorexia nervosa, bulimia nervosa and binge eating disorder. Please note that whilst I think it's helpful to understand the diagnostic criteria of major eating disorders, I also think that we must take care not to dismiss our concerns about young people who are not suffering with a diagnosable eating disorder. Many young people may either present with an atypical pattern of symptoms, or may be in the early stages of developing an eating disorder and not yet have reached diagnostic levels. In either instance, we should be offering the young person concerned appropriate support regardless of how well they fit with the diagnostic categories presented over the next few pages.

Anorexia nervosa

Anorexia nervosa, commonly referred to simply as 'anorexia', is the most fatal of all mental health disorders with up to 10 per cent of sufferers dying either as a result of suicide or, more commonly, due to complicating factors arising from low weight, such as organ failure or heart attack.

The most apparent symptom of anorexia is low weight – people with anorexia are usually keenly aware of the minimum weight recommendation for their height and will work very hard to keep below this weight. Despite their low weight, many people with anorexia will try to lose more weight by restricting their diet and/or exercising or will be very reluctant to gain weight even if they understand that their weight is abnormally low and putting them in medical danger. Additionally, they tend to have a completely distorted view of their body and genuinely believe they are fat or even obese. The easiest way to try to understand it is that it is like looking in a fairground mirror that distorts your shape. People with anorexia will be looking in the 'fat mirror' by default and have a constantly distorted view of their shape. Additionally, whilst they might be dangerously underweight, people with anorexia tend to be terrified of eating and gaining weight, even if this won't bring them close to the normal weight category for their height and age.

> 'The thinner I got, the fatter I felt. The pounds were dropping off, but each time I looked in the mirror I could see another roll of fat forming.'

Historically, cessation of menstrual periods in girls was a diagnostic criterion for anorexia. This is no longer the case but it is still worth being aware that where weight loss is extreme girls may have very irregular periods and may cease to have periods altogether unless they are taking the contraceptive pill. Younger girls will generally not start to menstruate if their weight is low.

People with anorexia tend to use their weight and shape as a way of evaluating themselves. They consider being fat to be bad and, although they are not fat, they think they are and will therefore tend to have very negative feelings about themselves and suffer from very low self-esteem. It's common for people with anorexia to weigh or measure themselves very regularly and their mood often directly reflects how 'well' they are doing with their weight loss. For example, it would not be uncommon for a girl with anorexia to arrive at morning registration in a particularly sad or angry mood if she found she had not lost weight that morning; she might be experiencing feelings of shame, failure and worthlessness. However, if she found she had lost weight that morning, she might arrive at registration in a lighter, more determined mood due to her perceived weight loss 'success'.

> 'If I'd gained like half a pound, I'd assume everyone was pointing and laughing at the fat girl. It was so hard to force myself to go to school and face the world those days.'

Many people with anorexia know the calorie content and/or nutritional breakdown of hundreds of foods. It is common for people with anorexia to set themselves a calorie limit for the day and obsessively count exactly how many calories they consume. If they consume more than the allotted amount of calories, they suffer immense feelings of guilt and shame and will often try to burn off calories by exercising. In fact, many students suffering with anorexia will keep themselves constantly moving and may insist on standing instead of sitting as it burns more calories, or may constantly jiggle their arms or legs or walk on the spot. Whilst we'd expect extreme weight loss to lead to lethargy, the opposite is true and people with extreme anorexia will often have the motivation and ability to exercise very hard – perhaps as a result of evolution: when humans lived a hunter-gatherer lifestyle in the past, at times when food was in short supply, we would have needed to expend more energy sourcing food before we succumbed to starvation.

Bulimia nervosa

The defining characteristic of bulimia is the binge–purge cycle (see Figure 1.1). A typical pattern is for a sufferer to consume a large quantity of food in a very short period of time. This is called bingeing. The type of food varies from person to person but is frequently very unhealthy food such as chocolates, crisps and cakes, though it can be just about anything the sufferer can lay their hands on. After the binge, the sufferer will try to remove the calories from their body. This is called purging. Purging can take many different forms: most frequently sufferers will make themselves vomit or will abuse laxatives or diuretics or compulsively exercise. Bulimia usually starts with dieting – and this is almost a 'default' setting, but when there is a slip in the diet, or a stressful situation arises and food is sought for comfort, this will often trigger a binge which in turn triggers a purge. Bulimia is typically quite cyclical, though the frequency of the cycle can vary from several times a day to every few weeks.

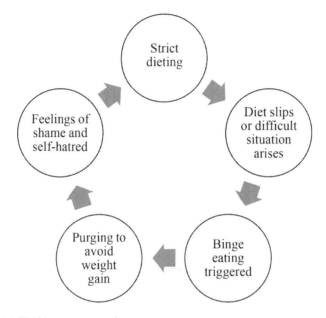

Figure 1.1: The binge–purge cycle

As only about 50 per cent of calories are generally expelled via purging, it does not tend to work as an effective weight-loss tool, but may prevent the weight gain which would otherwise result from bingeing. The result of this is that many people with bulimia maintain a roughly average weight, making the illness incredibly hard to detect. However, some bulimics will experience fluctuations in their weight, as they may gain weight during difficult periods when they are binging and purging heavily, and lose a little weight when they are binging and purging less or restricting their food intake heavily.

> 'I was on a diet ever since I could remember. It never worked because I wasn't very good at sticking to it. When I started taking laxatives I thought I'd found a magic bullet, but it didn't work out that way as I started bingeing more and more often and on larger and larger quantities of food. It was like, now I had a way to get rid of the food, it was okay to eat it. But it wasn't. I was

miserable when I was bingeing. I was miserable when I was purging and I
was miserable in between times too. It was an awful time.'

Like people with anorexia, people with bulimia tend to suffer from very
low self-esteem and attach a huge importance to their shape and weight.
They too tend to consider themselves too fat regardless of how fat or thin
they are and they use purging in order to try and control their weight.

Binge eating disorder

Binge eating disorder, sometimes referred to as compulsive eating or
emotional overeating, is a disorder typically characterized by a pattern
of eating large quantities of, often unhealthy, food over a short period
of time, usually within about two hours. It is very similar to bulimia, the
key difference being that sufferers do not purge after binging. This is the
reason why compulsive eaters tend to be overweight whereas bulimics
tend to be closer to a normal weight.

Binges tend to involve consuming unhealthy food very rapidly
and are associated with a feeling of loss of control. Bingeing usually
happens in secret and many people suffering with binge eating will make
efforts to control their diet outside of binges – so a young person who
is apparently eating healthily but whose weight is increasing constantly
may be secretly bingeing.

Binge eating is often dismissed simply as greed. This is not the case.
Binge eating is an eating disorder and its sufferers need just as much help
and support as people suffering from bulimia or anorexia.

'I felt like I'd succumbed to the wrong eating disorder. If I'd have had the
strength to starve myself then people would have cared. With every pound
you lose, they care about you more. But when you're gaining weight no
one stops to think "Hey, I wonder if she's okay," they just think "fat cow" and
walk on.'

As binge eaters consume large volumes of food but do not purge, they tend
to be overweight. In some cases they will be very overweight or obese
and their weight is likely to continually increase until the underlying
issues are addressed. This weight gain will usually be far in excess of the
usual weight gain you'd expect to see in a growing child.

When talking about their binges, binge eaters will often refer to a
lack of control and a complete inability to stop themselves eating, almost
as if their body is working on remote control during a binge and they
can't press the stop button. Binges tend to happen in secret with the
sufferer often making attempts at a healthy diet outside of their binges

in order to control their weight. A student whose weight is increasing despite apparently healthy eating habits could be secretly bingeing.

As with anorexia and bulimia, binge eaters tend to suffer from very low self-esteem, which is frequently exacerbated by the teasing, bullying and social stigma that is commonly experienced by people who are overweight. This can be a vicious cycle as sufferers' low self-esteem will drive them to eat compulsively and the resulting weight gain will lower their self-esteem further. In most cases, they are aware there is a problem and are often desperate to address it but are completely unable to do so without help and support to address their underlying issues.

Other eating disorders

In addition to the three major eating disorders, individuals can be diagnosed with Other Specified Feeding or Eating Disorder (OSFED – formerly known as Eating Disorder Not Otherwise Specified or 'EDNOS'). OSFED is a diagnosis that is applied to patients who do not meet the diagnostic criteria for one of the three major eating disorders, though this diagnosis is not an indication of a less severe eating disorder, but rather a different combination of symptoms. This is a relatively frequent occurrence as people with eating disorders do not always neatly fit into diagnostic categories and may suffer from symptoms or behaviours typical of more than one of the disorders without reaching the diagnostic criteria for any single disorder.

Whilst it's important to understand the different forms eating disorders can take, I would suggest you forget about the labels and aim to support anyone who is suffering from an eating disorder *or* eating disorder-like tendencies – early support for someone with a subclinical eating disorder can often prevent them from developing a full-blown eating disorder.

Eating problems specific to under-11s

Children under 11 can develop a wide range of food difficulties in addition to the eating disorders outlined above. These patterns of food behaviour may persist into the teenage years and are more lilkely to do so when a student has special or additional needs. Common difficulties include:

- food refusal
- restrictive eating

- selective eating

- food phobia

- food avoidance emotional disorder.

These difficulties are not all well understood and are commonly misdiagnosed. It's important also to remember that many children will experience difficulties that don't fit neatly into one category or another, but these classifications will help you to gain some understanding of the range of behaviours you could encounter when working with younger children or older children with special or additional needs.

Food refusal

Food refusal is commonly found in pre-school children, where the refusal of food can be used as a way to communicate a message or for a child to 'get their own way'. However, this can persist in slightly older children, where the main feature is an inconsistent refusal of food. These children will tend to eat their favourite foods without any problem at all and may refuse food only when they are with particular people or in a particular situation – for example, refusing to eat at school but eating normally at home or vice versa.

Worry or unhappiness underlies the food refusal in many cases, but the child may not have the capacity to express their concerns using language. These children are usually of normal weight and height, and this problem does not usually pose a threat to the child's health.

> 'It took us a while, but eventually we understood that he was trying to tell us something by refusing to eat or drink at school. It turned out he was being teased by the other kids at school about his lisp.'

Restrictive eating

These children eat smaller amounts of food than they should do for their age. Their diet is normal in terms of the range of food eaten and the nutrients that it contains and is unusual only in terms of the volume of food consumed. Restrictive eaters are often thin compared to their peers and they tend to be short, but otherwise they generally seem healthy and happy. It's common for other members of the family to have a history of the same pattern of food intake.

Selective eating

The most obvious feature of this condition is the narrow range of food that is eaten – it is sometimes referred to as 'extreme faddiness'. This can persist for months or even years. Selective eaters are very unwilling to try new types of food and the behaviour of these children, which is usually normal, is likely to deteriorate if they feel that they are being forced to eat a wider range of foods than they feel comfortable with. Social problems may start to occur beyond the age of about five because selective eating causes difficulties when attending birthday parties or visiting a friend's house.

Additionally, children who eat only a restricted sugary diet may have problems with their teeth. The weight of these children does not give much of an indication as to whether there is a problem – they may be of low, normal or high weight.

Food phobia

Children who have developed food phobias are typically very resistant to eating and drinking, which can cause a great deal of concern. Food phobias are typically developed following a choking or vomiting incident and sufferers tend to avoid foods that have certain textures because they think they will choke, gag or be sick. Some children with food phobias will claim that eating and drinking hurts. Mealtimes often turn into a battleground. The majority of these children do, however, seem to grow and develop because the food and drink that they are willing to consume provides enough calories and nutrients.

> 'He was convinced that if he ate he would be poisoned. He got thinner and thinner. At first we thought he needed treatment for anorexia, but in fact he needed talking therapy to overcome his phobia, which started after some food gave him vomiting and diarrhoea on holiday.'

Food avoidance emotional disorder

Children with food avoidance emotional disorder experience a loss of appetite which is usually associated with depression or anxiety and may follow a traumatic incident such as a bereavement. There is often a more general disturbance in behaviour that does not centre on food and mealtimes; for example, in addition to a loss of appetite the child may experience problems with sleeping, poor concentration, tearfulness and a general sense of hopelessness.

Food avoidance emotional disorder is sometimes mistakenly diagnosed as anorexia as these children tend to become very underweight. However, a key distinguishing feature is that, unlike children with anorexia, those with food avoidance emotional disorder recognize that they are underweight and often express a desire to eat more but they simply cannot bring themselves to do so.

> 'She was only seven, but you could tell just by looking at her that her spirit was broken. Her father was dying and she had lost the will to carry on. She hated that she was worrying everyone by getting thinner but each time she tried to eat, she just broke down in tears.'

IS IT A PROBLEM?

Eating difficulties in children under 11 and the special needs population are relatively commonplace. Whilst some issues are passing phases and present no real threat to the child's physical or emotional wellbeing, some cases do require professional support. If a child is displaying unusual behaviour around food, and you're not sure if you need extra help, ask yourself:

- Are they taking in enough calories/nutrients so that they are not hungry?

- Are they growing normally?

- Do they seem happy and healthy in themselves?

If you can answer 'yes' to each of these questions then the behaviour should be monitored but there is no cause for alarm. It is quite normal for children to go through phases with food and most will simply pass with time. However, if you begin to become concerned about the child's health or wellbeing then you will need to act. In many cases, the child is trying to communicate something that they do not have the skills, language or confidence to communicate, and trying to find alternative methods for the child to communicate their concerns – for example, through art therapy or play therapy – can be the key to overcoming their unusual food-related behaviours.

Self-harm explained

A generally accepted definition of self-harm is causing harm to one's own body, usually through physical abuse. Self-harm is usually conducted at times of anger, distress, fear, worry, depression or low self-esteem in order to manage negative feelings. Self-harm can also be used as a form of self-punishment for something that the self-harmer has done, thinks they have done, are told by someone else that they have done or feel they have allowed to be done to themselves.

Common forms of self-harm

Self-harm takes many different forms, but by far the most common type of self-harm we see in adolescents is cutting, followed by burning, aggressive behaviours (punching walls or doors in anger) and self-poisoning (taking non-lethal overdoses). Amongst younger children and the special needs population, the most common forms of self-harm are bruising/battering, hair-pulling, scratching and picking, including not allowing wounds to heal. Some behaviours, such as hair-pulling and scratching, can start out as a deliberate act but become a compulsive habit over time.

Indirect self-harm

There are further behaviours which do not fall neatly under the category of self-harm, but which may indicate similar underlying issues and which you may choose to respond to in the same way as more clear-cut forms of self-harm. These behaviours are sometimes referred to as 'indirect self-harm' and include:

- substance misuse through excessive alcohol or drug consumption

- eating disorders

- physical risk-taking

- sexual risk-taking

- self-neglect

- misuse of prescribed medication (this is relatively common in adolescents with diabetes).

In particular, schools are reporting a rapid rise in the number of adolescent girls repeatedly entering into relationships in which they are sexually, physically or emotionally abused. Some forms of indirect self-harm present a direct safeguarding risk. In these cases, a referral to the child and family assessment team (CAFAT) or equivalent may provide additional support to the young person and their family.

TERMS USED TO DESCRIBE SELF-HARM

You may hear a wide variety of terms used to refer to self-harm including:

- self-harm

- deliberate self-harm

- intentional self-harm

- parasuicide

- attempted suicide

- non-fatal suicidal behaviour

- self-inflicted violence.

Increasingly we tend not to use terms like 'deliberate' or 'intentional' as these terms are felt to place a negative value judgement on the individual concerned and also infer intent and control where this is not always the case.

Self-harm is sometimes considered to include three subtypes:

- self-poisoning

- self-injury

- self-mutilation.

Severity of behaviours

It is common for people to believe that the severity of a student's self-harming or eating-disordered behaviour is a direct reflection of the severity of the underlying psychological difficulties they are trying to cope with. Whilst this is sometimes the case, it is not always so and it is inappropriate for us to dismiss less serious cases out of hand. In some instances, students will even lie about carrying out self-harming or eating-disordered behaviours, pretending that they are self-harming and perhaps even sharing images sourced online of others' self-harm and passing it off as their own. This should not be dismissed as 'attention-seeking' – this student is seeking your attention in an unusual way, but they are clearly indicating that they are in need of support. Students whose invented or lower-level issues are not offered the appropriate support often go on to carry out more extreme behaviours in order both to cope with their underlying issues and/or to help them to access the support they are in need of.

Self-harm and suicide

Self-harm and suicide are often considered under the same umbrella. In fact, the National Collaborating Centre for Mental Health guidelines[1] use the definition 'Self-poisoning or self-injury, irrespective of the apparent purpose of the act' to describe self-harm – which means that someone would be considered to be self-harming even when their intention was to take their own life.

In this book, I approach self-harm separately to acts with suicidal intent because my work with students leads me to understand that these are two very different types of behaviour. In fact many students express the belief that self-harm is the one thing that helps them to cope with day-to-day life enough not to contemplate suicide.

> 'I would get overwhelmed and feel like I didn't want to be alive any more, but cutting would help me to calm down. It stopped me doing something even more stupid.'

It can, however, sometimes be hard to differentiate between self-harm and suicide attempts. For example, imagine two students who arrive at a hospital: 15-year-old Jenna has taken 20 painkillers whilst 17-year-old Ranj has life-threatening cuts to his arms. Are these examples of self-harm or are they suicide attempts? The only way we can gain any real insight is to ask the student about their intention at the time when the behaviour was taking place. However, they may not be able to remember, may feel ambivalent or may find it difficult to articulate their reasons.

Many people self-harm for months or even years without ever feeling suicidal. Self-harm is a separate behaviour from suicide and the intent is to cope with feelings rather than to end life. However, if people who self-harm don't receive the support and help they need to overcome their underlying difficulties, they may go on to contemplate suicide later on.

If you are at all concerned that a student is feeling suicidal you should seek help immediately. When people suffer with suicidal feelings they can often feel very alone and they are very, very vulnerable. You should also seek immediate help for students with severe physical injuries, whether or not you believe they intended to take their own life.

---

1   National Collaborating Centre for Mental Health (2004) *Eating Disorders: Core Interventions in the Treatment and Management of Anorexia Nervosa, Bulimia Nervosa and Related Eating Disorders.* NICE Clinical Guideline 9. London: The British Psychological Society and Gaskell.

LEARNING TO TAKE AWAY FROM THIS CHAPTER

- Whilst different eating disorders may have a markedly different impact on the sufferer's appearance, the underlying thoughts, feelings and psychological distress are often very similar.

- There are three major eating disorders: anorexia nervosa, bulimia nervosa and binge eating disorder. Many young people with food and weight concerns will not fit within the criteria for these disorders, but it is still important that we offer our full support.

- Children under 11 often use food to express concerns/feelings they do not have the language to articulate.

- With common childhood issues such as 'faddiness', if the child is growing normally, is not hungry and is happy then there is often no need for concern.

- Self-harm is an unhealthy coping mechanism students may use to manage difficult feelings or emotions and can be carried out in a variety of ways.

- Most people who self-harm have no suicidal intent. Many people who self-harm express the belief that self-harming protects them from taking more serious measures.

CHAPTER 2

Overcoming Stigma and Exploring Common Misconceptions

This chapter will enable you to:

- increase staff confidence in talking about self-harm and eating disorders
- correct common misconceptions about self-harm and eating disorders
- run parent workshops and information sessions.

Many school staff that I've worked with have told me that in their school topics like eating disorders or self-harm were taboo, either because the school was uncomfortable admitting there was a problem or because there was concern that talking about eating disorders or self-harm would lead to a rise in cases. Other staff simply feel understandably uncomfortable or out of their depth when talking about mental health and emotional wellbeing issues so they end up avoiding the topic.

In order to effectively support students with self-harming or eating-disordered behaviours at your school or college, it's important that the taboo is tackled. It's important that we get more comfortable discussing these topics; not doing so can cost lives:

> 'Everything came to a head one day when she collapsed at school. She was rushed to hospital but there was nothing they could do. She died of a heart attack. It turned out that several members of staff, myself included, had been worried about her, but we all assumed that someone else was taking care of it – it wasn't exactly the kind of thing we discussed in the staffroom.'

Increasing staff confidence in talking about sensitive issues

Staff feeling comfortable talking about eating disorders and self-harm can prevent students falling through the gaps and ensure that cases are picked up. A series of ideas that your school or college could consider implementing to tackle stigma and get people talking about self-harm and eating disorders are explored below.

Offer all staff relevant training

Some members of staff are likely to need more extensive training than others due to differing roles but, as a minimum, all members of staff should have a basic understanding of what eating disorders and self-harm are and some of the warning signs to look out for. This could be done in as little as an hour. This hour-long investment will mean staff feel more confident discussing eating disorders and self-harm and may be able to spot potential cases before they develop into something more serious.

Let staff know how they can offer proactive support to sufferers

This is especially important when you have known cases of eating disorders or self-harm in school, or where you have a student who has returned from treatment. Staff can often feel very uncomfortable, with little idea of how to help. By sharing really practical ideas and strategies with them, you will help them to realize that they are able to offer an important input and are in a great position to support the student.

Have a clear policy

Your school should have clear policies and procedures in place for responding to cases of self-harm and eating disorders. These may be discrete policies or they may form part of another policy, for example, your child protection or safeguarding policy. Wherever this information resides, the key thing is that roles and responsibilities should be made very clear and all staff should know who to refer their concerns on to if they suspect that a child may be suffering from self-harm or an eating disorder. In schools where no one talks about eating disorders or self-harm and there is no clear policy or procedures being implemented, cases will often fall through the cracks until they have reached a critical stage.

'I suspected he was self-harming, all the tell-tale signs were there, but naively I thought that someone else was dealing with it and that it wasn't my place to become involved. It was weeks and weeks after my first suspicions that he spoke to me about his difficulties and it became clear he was not receiving any support. I felt incredibly guilty about all that time he'd been suffering alone and I'd just stood by and done nothing to help.'

Routinely talk about mental health and emotional wellbeing concerns
In meetings where you address behavioural and academic concerns about students, try and introduce the idea of also discussing any mental health or emotional wellbeing concerns you have. By talking about concerns early on and in a forum where there are other members of staff who may be able to help contribute to the whole picture, you put yourself in a good position to pick up cases early and provide the support that's needed at a point when it is most likely to be accepted and effective.

> 'It felt a bit weird at first because we were more used to talking about academic performance and bad behaviour, but we soon got used to mentioning kids whose wellbeing was a cause for concern and it turned out to be a great forum for it too. You'd be surprised how often kids who start struggling academically or whose behaviour has deteriorated have an underlying problem with their mental health or wellbeing. If you can get to the bottom of that and help them to address it, their grades and their behaviour seem to follow.'

As well as enabling you to identify cases, routinely talking about concerns about student wellbeing will make all staff feel more comfortable talking about these issues. It will also raise awareness about the risk factors and warning signs that all staff should be on the lookout for.

Common misconceptions about self-harm and eating disorders

There are many widely perpetuated myths about self-harm and eating disorders. Taking time to understand these misconceptions and dispel those myths within the staff and student body can be a key way to address the stigma associated with self-harm and eating disorders as well as other mental health and emotional wellbeing issues.

You may choose to take a targeted approach to dispelling myths, or simply to ensure that you have the knowledge and information you need to tackle them head on as you hear them at school. Either way, making an effort to correct people's misconceptions can play a key part in providing a more understanding and accepting climate for those students who are attempting to overcome their own self-harming or eating disorder difficulties.

*Myth: Eating disorders are a result of vanity
and are caused by the media*

It is commonly believed that people with anorexia are starving themselves in a pursuit of thinness and beauty and that these behaviours are caused by the Photoshopped images we are all bombarded with daily in magazines, online, on TV, on billboards – everywhere we look.

It's true that being surrounded by the 'thin ideal' and images of unobtainable beauty can lower our self-esteem and make us strive for perfection and may contribute to the early stages of an eating disorder, but eating disorders are serious mental health issues which go far beyond diet and vanity. With a full-blown eating disorder, the sufferer's food, weight and shape are used as a coping mechanism – that might mean depriving themselves of food, or it might mean bingeing on food to comfort themselves or in response to difficult circumstances. A desire to be thin and beautiful, and the images we see in the media, may contribute towards the development of an eating disorder – but they are far from the sole factor. In fact some people develop eating disorders in order to try and make themselves look ugly. It is quite common for victims of rape or other abuse to under- or overeat either consciously or subconsciously in order to make themselves less attractive. Additionally, there are many documented cases of anorexia in blind people.

> 'It frustrates me when people assume that eating disorders are all about appearances. We're a blind school and have had several cases of anorexia over the years, all in kids who were born unable to see. They've never been exposed to the media like their peers, yet they starve themselves. They never talk about what they look like – my understanding is that they are using food as a way of taking control of their lives.'

Myth: Self-harm and eating disorders are attention-seeking behaviours

Eating disorders are generally very secretive diseases. People with bulimia can go undetected for many years unless they seek help, whilst people with binge eating disorder often go to great lengths to eat healthily in the company of others and binge only in private. People who are severely anorexic tend to attract a certain amount of attention due to their emaciated appearance, but this attention is often misinterpreted, with the sufferer genuinely believing that people are staring at them because they are fat rather than realizing it is because they are thin.

Self-harm tends to fall into two broad camps: those who hide their injuries and those who don't. Those who hide their injuries will often harm parts of the body which are least likely to be detected, such as the stomach or the tops of their arms and legs. These cases can go undetected indefinitely, often only coming to our attention if a disclosure is made. Conversely, some people who self-harm will not attempt to hide their injuries and may be judged as 'flaunting' them. Rather than dismissing this as attention-seeking behaviour, we should stop and ask ourselves 'Why is this student seeking attention? What are they trying to communicate?' For some students, unable to communicate or seek help for emotional or psychological trauma they have experienced, their only means of seeking help is through a physical injury. Instead of 'attention seeking' a more useful way to consider this behaviour is 'attention needing' – encourage colleagues not to be so quick to judge but rather to consider what support the individual needs.

People suffering with self-harm and eating disorders routinely suffer from self-esteem that is so low that they can't believe that anyone would ever care about them – attention seeking is often the last thing on their mind.

> 'I would have probably asked for some help sooner if I hadn't thought my cutting would just be written off as attention seeking. Knowing that people would judge me like that made me very reluctant to talk about what was happening.'

Myth: People who binge eat should just eat less and exercise more

Binge eaters have received a bad press for a long time. They are unfairly viewed by many as fat and lazy people who should take control of their diet and try to eat and act more healthily. However, it's not that simple. For someone who suffers from binge eating disorder, food is often the only mechanism they have for dealing with their emotions and the difficulties they face in their day-to-day lives. Food is like a drug to them; it numbs their pain. They know that they should stop bingeing and will often be thinking about the fact that they shouldn't binge even as they prepare to do so. However, they tend to lose all control when they're eating – binge eaters often talk about feeling almost like they're being possessed whilst they're bingeing. They want to eat less, they want to lose weight but they simply can't do it until they receive the support they need to learn new coping mechanisms or overcome their underlying difficulties.

Myth: People who self-harm are suicidal

Many people believe that all acts of self-harm have suicidal intent behind then. This belief is particularly strong in cases where a student uses cutting as a coping mechanism or takes a non-lethal overdose. This belief can lead to hysterical reactions to disclosures of self-harm. Whilst students who self-harm are more at risk of going on to contemplate suicide than their peers, especially if their underlying issues are not dealt with, about 90 per cent of students who self-harm never contemplate suicide. In fact, many students talk about self-harm as a protective factor against suicide. When self-harm is used as a coping strategy to keep emotions and feelings in check, it can prevent difficulties from escalating to the point where they feel the need to take their own life.

> 'I felt like a balloon. All my emotions made the balloon blow up bigger and bigger. When I self-harmed it was like letting a little bit of air out of the balloon. If I didn't cut, I'm pretty sure that before too long the balloon would have popped.'

Myth: You can tell if someone has an eating disorder by looking at them

People with eating disorders can be any size or shape. They may be underweight, average weight or overweight. Somebody's weight and appearance is a symptom of their eating disorder and it takes time to lose or gain a lot of weight. Somebody who has recently developed anorexia or binge eating disorder may be completely gripped by the terrifying thoughts and feelings that accompany these disorders without, yet, having experienced significant weight loss or gain. Many people who suffer with bulimia maintain a roughly normal weight so the disorder can be impossible to detect simply by appearance alone at any stage in their illness.

Myth: Eating disorders are a lifestyle choice; sufferers can choose to stop

Eating disorders are not a lifestyle choice, they are serious mental health conditions which can completely take over an individual's ability to make reasoned decisions. There are many online websites, blogs and forums which promote anorexia and bulimia as lifestyle choices, where sufferers provide each other with support and share tips for weight loss and purging. These sites can significantly contribute to sufferers' decline, normalizing their illness and causing it to become more and more severe.

Myth: It's easy to stop self-harming

Many sufferers describe self-harm as an addiction and find the cycle very difficult to break as they have no other means of coping with their overwhelming thoughts and feelings other than hurting themselves.

However, people who have not self-harmed do not understand the complex emotions and psychology underpinning each act of self-harm and assume it would be easy to stop. This is not the case, and expecting somebody to suddenly stop self-harming can be very dangerous. If we remove this means of coping then they may find themselves in a more desperate situation; it is at these moments that a sufferer's thoughts are more likely to turn to suicide. Generally speaking, students who are suffering from either self-harm or an eating disorder find it difficult to stop unless there is a significant change in their underlying circumstances, or unless they receive support to develop healthier coping mechanisms and come to terms with their difficulties.

Myth: Eating disorders are a teenage phase

Eating disorders are not a phase. Sufferers rarely recover without significant support to develop healthier coping mechanisms and to address any underlying issues which may have triggered their eating disorder. Additionally, whilst the peak age of onset of eating disorders is between the ages of about 13 and 20, they can affect people of any age, including very young children and the elderly.

Myth: People who self-harm are crazy

People who have never self-harmed find it very difficult to understand why somebody would purposefully hurt themselves and think that there must be something very wrong with someone who would choose to do so. However, we find it far easier to understand somebody coping with their emotions by eating junk food or drinking alcohol. Self-harm is simply an alternative coping mechanism and does not mean that someone is psychotic or crazy, as people often think.

> 'I think everyone thought I was insane and should be locked up. They couldn't understand my need to burn myself. I couldn't understand why they felt a need to smoke marijuana. Their form of self-medication and self-harm was far more accepted than mine though.'

Myth: Purging is an effective way to lose weight

People with bulimia have a cycle of bingeing on large amounts of food and then ridding themselves of that food through different purging mechanisms – generally self-induced vomiting or laxative abuse. This tends to result in weight maintenance rather than weight loss as most purging mechanisms will rid the body of only about 50 per cent of the calories that have been consumed. Laxative abuse tends to result in dehydration which can give the illusion of weight loss, but this is temporary.

Myth: People who self-harm don't feel pain

People often mistakenly assume that people who injure themselves intentionally are unable to feel pain or that they seek pleasure in pain, otherwise they surely would not choose to do it. However, there is no evidence that people who injure themselves feel pain any differently to anybody else. Many people who self-harm do so specifically so that they can feel pain, because underlying issues such as depression may have left them feeling entirely numb and so they are left wanting to feel something to remind them they're alive, even if that means suffering pain as a consequence.

> 'Of course it hurt! It really hurt. That was good – I didn't like the pain exactly, but I did like the fact that just for a few moments I could feel. Those moments of physical pain helped me to feel a part of the world for a few minutes. The rest of the time I felt so numb and disjointed it was like I was floating around in a big black bubble.'

Myth: Eating disorders aren't life threatening

Eating disorders can be fatal; approximately 10 per cent of people with anorexia die either as a complication of the disease (e.g. organ failure) or as a result of suicide. In addition to the risk of suicide and fatal complications of the illness, all three of the major eating disorders can result in long-term physical damage being caused to the body which can affect sufferers for the rest of their lives. However, many people go on to make a full physical recovery.

Myth: You can't recover from an eating disorder

There are two schools of thought on this. Many people believe that eating disorders are like the common perception of alcoholism and that, once you have suffered, you have to make a positive decision to eat healthily every day for the rest of your life. Others believe that it is possible to make a complete recovery. Either way, it is perfectly possible for someone with an eating disorder to go on to live a completely normal and happy life, especially if their illness is picked up in the early stages.

> 'I wouldn't say it's gone. But it's been a decade now since I had any symptoms. I make a decision to eat healthily every day – that's an easy decision these days. That said, if something really terrible happened to me today, I can't 100 per cent promise I'd eat dinner…'

It is common for people with eating disorders to relapse repeatedly during their initial recovery period whilst they learn to employ healthier coping mechanisms. Learning to spot the early warning signs of relapse and to respond appropriately is often considered a key aspect of recovery.

Some people suffer with eating disorders for years, decades or their whole life, whilst others recover for a very long period and then relapse after many years as a result of trauma, for example. There are examples of people who have suffered from disordered eating for several decades but have gone on to make a full recovery. The author June Alexander, for instance, who tells her story of four decades of eating disorders in her memoir *A Boy Called Tim* and has gone on to recover fully and become an advocate for eating disorder recovery.

Myth: Self-harm and eating disorders only affect girls

The highest rate of onset of eating disorders is in females aged 13 to 20 but it's important that we do not allow this stereotype to make us blind to other cases of the disorders. Approximately one in ten patients diagnosed with anorexia is male. Eating disorders do not discriminate and can affect anyone. They occur across all cultural and socio-economic backgrounds, amongst people of all ages, from children to the elderly, and in both males and females.

Similarly, self-harm is often viewed as a predominantly female phenomenon, but many males self-harm too – though some of the methods they use may not always be automatically considered self-harm. For instance, a boy who vents his anger and frustration by getting into fights or doing himself harm whilst punching and kicking walls, doors and furniture may be written off as an aggressive adolescent, but if this behaviour is regularly repeated and is the boy's only means of coping with his feelings then there is an argument for considering it as a form of self-harm. Additionally, boys tend to be a lot more reluctant to talk about their problems and will go to greater lengths to keep symptoms of self-harm and eating disorders hidden than their female counterparts, which also helps to perpetuate the myth that very few boys are affected. The truth is that many boys are affected both by self-harm and eating disorders but are often suffering in silence rather than having their need for support met.

> 'It kind of sucks being a boy who self-harms. You're like some sort of freakish oddity. I don't think I'm half as unusual as people think though, I think I'm just the one who feels a little bit happier talking about it, and the rest are hiding.'

Running parent workshops and information sessions

As well as breaking down the taboo with staff, it can be helpful to get parents talking too. A great way to help forge links between parents and the school or college is to hold information evenings or workshops for parents which allow them to learn basic information about issues such as self-harm or eating disorders. This can both reinforce the importance to parents of informing and working with the school if they have concerns about their child and also be a good vehicle to provide parents with information about the support that is available at school and to reinforce the message that no child at your school will ever be discriminated against on the basis of mental health or emotional wellbeing issues.

More than anything, parents will often welcome the opportunity to discuss their concerns and to talk with other parents about their experiences or worries. You do not need a long session to have a big impact and it is often helpful to keep the atmosphere relatively light-hearted by providing refreshments. Within the session, you could cover:

- explanation of/information about the particular mental health issue(s) you've chosen to focus on

- details or warning signs

- exploration of the limits of 'normal' adolescent behaviour – at what point should a parent worry?

- clear guidance on who parents can talk to at school about their concerns

- information about the support available at or via the school

- details of further sources of information.

It is also helpful if you can provide parents with suggested guidance about what to do if a friend of their child confides in them about their difficulties, or if their child expresses concern about a friend. This can put parents in a very difficult situation as they may not know how best to help whilst feeling a huge pressure to do the right thing. Children are more likely to confide in a friend's parents than their own so it really is worth discussing this issue with parents. When discussing this with parents you might like to consider:

- discussing the importance of not promising the child confidentiality as they are likely to break this promise which may jeopardize their relationship with the child

- considering what they should do next – for example, discussing the issue with the parents of the child concerned, or the school, or both

- discussing how they can be supportive moving forwards.

'We were worried that no one would turn up. We had the opposite problem, there weren't enough seats! We had planned a half hour presentation with ten minutes for questions. The questions ended up extending to over an hour. We had some fantastic feedback; more than anything parents were just grateful to feel less alone and to talk about issues that had felt so taboo. In the days following, we had several parents contact us with concerns about their children so we were able to feel a very real and immediate impact.'

LEARNING TO TAKE AWAY FROM THIS CHAPTER

- The key ways to break down the stigma and taboo surrounding eating disorders and self-harm is to promote discussion and learning.

- It is important to have clear policies, procedures and lines of responsibility in place, otherwise vulnerable students may go unsupported.

- There are many misconceptions perpetuated about self-harm and eating disorders. These are often stigmatizing and may prevent a student in need from seeking the help and support they need.

- Parents often welcome the opportunity to learn more about mental health and emotional wellbeing issues from the school.

- Parents may be concerned about how to provide support to their son or daughter's friends.

THINGS TO DO

- Ensure that every member of your school staff has received at least basic training about self-harm and eating disorders.

- Ensure every member of staff knows to whom they should refer concerns about a student.

- Actively address misconceptions about self-harm and eating disorders as you come across them at school.

- Organize an information and discussion evening for parents.

CHAPTER 3

Teaching Students about Self-Harm and Eating Disorders

This chapter will enable you to:

- understand the benefits and risks of teaching students about self-harm and eating disorders
- utilize ground rules designed to promote a culture of safe exploration
- implement safeguards to ensure the wellbeing of vulnerable students
- confidently develop student understanding without promoting unsafe behaviours.

There is a much perpetrated myth that teaching students about self-harm or eating disorders will make them many times more likely to develop these issues. Teaching students about eating disorders and self-harm may make the incidence of eating disorders appear to increase within your school, but that is because cases which would have previously gone unrecognized may now be picked up. That is a good thing as it means these students who had previously slipped below the radar are now receiving much-needed support. However, in order to do no harm, these topics must be approached carefully and sensitively within the context of a broader developmental curriculum. Ideas for this are outlined in the following pages.

A key benefit of taking the time to teach your students about eating disorders and self-harm is that this will make them realize that you think these issues are important topics worth talking about and which you are not scared to discuss openly. It will also help them to realize that you are knowledgeable on the topic, as long as you have prepared appropriately. Two key barriers to students talking about their own or their friends' eating disorders to staff at school are that they believe that teachers do not understand eating disorders and will therefore be unable to help, and that they think that their teacher will think it's unimportant or that they are blowing things out of proportion. By teaching your students about eating disorders and self-harm you can quickly overcome these barriers and make students far more likely to confide in a member of school staff about any concerns they may have.

What age is appropriate?

I am often asked at what age it is appropriate to teach students about issues such as self-harm and eating disorders. I don't believe that there is a universal answer to this and you should always develop your scheme of work to suit the individual skills, knowledge and readiness of the young people you're working with. However, the following guidelines may prove helpful.

- If children are directly exposed to self-harm, suicide, eating disorders or their effects, for example, in a classmate, then I would prioritize teaching about the topic in an age-appropriate manner even if students are very young. This may require specialist support.

- As a general rule, I would wait to teach explicitly about self-harm or eating disorders until high school/secondary school. About age 12 is an appropriate time to begin to explore these topics with most children.

- The skills needed to prevent and manage unhealthy coping mechanisms including self-harm and eating disorders can be taught from an early age. Children as young as five or six will benefit from lessons which develop:

  - communication skills

  - problem-solving skills

  - healthy coping mechanisms

  - stress management

  - knowledge about where and how to seek help if needed.

- Many schools introduce lessons for the age group at which they see an increase in prevalence in issues such as self-harm (often around age 13 or 14 though this varies between settings). This is useful, but what is more useful is to introduce these lessons six months or a year prior to this age, as this will help to prevent the onset of these difficulties for some of your students. This learning can be reinforced and built on as students enter the peak age of onset.

- Finally, I think it's important for us to move away from the idea that these topics need to be fitted into the curriculum and taught once at an appropriate age. Preferably, students should develop their skills and knowledge over a period of several years within the context of a broader developmental curriculum.

What you should teach

You should teach students basic information about the major eating disorders or forms of self-harm and their warning signs. You should explore why people might develop these difficulties and try to tackle the stigma and taboo associated with mental health and emotional wellbeing issues. It's also very helpful to teach students about eating disorder and self-harm warning signs and give them some clear direction on where they can go for help and support if they are concerned about themselves or a friend.

What you should *not* do is go into too much detail about the technical details of self-harm or eating disorders as this could trigger unhealthy responses in any vulnerable individuals in your group. For example, those students already struggling with eating-disordered thoughts could have their existing condition exacerbated by:

- talking about specific weights – an eating-disordered student may try to 'beat' any weight you've talked about

- showing pictures which glamorize eating disorders – showing a lot of pictures of models who are 'too thin' may actually work as 'thinspiration' for students who may not find the images disturbing, but consider them beautiful and aspirational

- talking about specific weight-loss or purging techniques – a student who is struggling with an eating disorder may never have thought of, for example, taking laxatives to further control their weight until they heard the idea in your class. Make sure you're not providing a kind of 'how-to' guide.

Similarly, talking about specific methods of self-harm can be instructive to vulnerable students, so whilst you might choose to talk about different methods of self-harm which could include cutting and burning, I would not recommend talking about specific methods that students might employ for cutting or burning themselves as these suggestions may be taken on board by any students who are currently harming.

POTENTIAL LEARNING OUTCOMES

Students should learn about self-harm and eating disorders as part of a developmental curriculum rather than in a single catch-all lesson. Relevant learning outcomes that you might look to build into your lesson planning might promote students' understanding of:

- what self-harm and eating disorders are

- some of the reasons why people develop unhealthy coping mechanisms

- common misconceptions about mental health and emotional wellbeing difficulties

- warning signs to look out for in a friend

- how to be a supportive friend, including the importance of disclosure of concerns

- where and how to seek help if needed

- what happens next following a student disclosure at school

- using anonymous helplines to 'practise' preceding a face-to-face disclosure

- how to safely seek support online and avoid potential pitfalls

- what to do in an emergency.

More generally we can promote student wellbeing and help prevent students turning to unhealthy coping mechanisms by promoting learning about:

- healthy ways of managing difficult thoughts and feelings

- verbal and written communications skills

- problem-solving skills – both preventative and in response to difficulties

- promoting good physical and mental health

- looking after ourselves at times of high stress, for example, exam season.

All teaching and learning resources should be inclusive of different ethnicities, sexual orientations, gender identities and disabilities.

Students will value knowing how best to support a friend

You can also give students some guidance on how they could support a friend who is struggling with eating-disordered or self-harming behaviours, or who they are concerned may be developing a problem. They will really value this advice and will often act on it if they have concerns already. You should work hard to encourage students that one of the most supportive things they can do for a friend at risk is to inform a trusted adult at school or home. You may need to explore reasons why a student may or may not choose to do this. This can be a good opportunity to discuss any concerns students might have about talking to an adult when they are worried that a friend might be self-harming or have an eating disorder, and also to put straight any misconceptions whilst taking on board valuable feedback. You can teach students that they can support their friends by doing things such as:

- never allowing weight or appearance-related bullying or teasing

- being a good listener to their friend

- standing by their friend but allowing them a little distance if they need it

- forgiving their friend if they are rude, difficult or unsociable

- not complimenting their friends' weight or appearance – you can practise paying compliments using other attributes instead.

Utilizing ground rules to promote a culture of safe discussion

When teaching about topics such as self-harm and eating disorders, it is important to think carefully about the possibility of personal disclosures from students who, as a result of the lesson, may develop the skills, language, knowledge and understanding needed to make a disclosure about their own mental health or emotional wellbeing. Whilst this is not to be discouraged, it is very important that if students make personal disclosures to school staff, they do so in a suitable, one-to-one setting. It is not appropriate, therefore, to encourage students to talk about sensitive personal matters in the classroom.

Therefore, it's important that, before teaching about these issues, clear 'ground rules' are established or reinforced and the concepts of confidentiality and anonymity covered at the start of the lesson. Ground rules need to be consistently adhered to, regularly revisited and, if necessary, renegotiated and reinforced. The teacher should lead the way by modelling the ground rules in their own communications with the class.

Where time allows, ground rules are most effective when they have been negotiated and agreed with the students, rather than imposed by the teacher. Below are some areas to introduce if they do not arise naturally.

- Encourage openness.

- Distance the learning.

- Keep the conversation in the room.

- Maintain a non-judgemental approach.

- Ensure the right to pass.

- Make no assumptions.

- Listen to others.

- Use language carefully.

- Ask questions.

- Encourage seeking help and advice.

Encourage openness

An important part of breaking down the stigma that surrounds mental health issues is to encourage an ethos of openness but within specific boundaries. These should be governed by your school's safeguarding policy. Mental health should not be a taboo topic and it should be openly and honestly discussed within the classroom setting, which should feel like a safe and supportive environment for discussions on mental health that are positive and affirming whilst giving students the opportunity to share their concerns. However, it needs to be agreed with students that lesson time is not the appropriate setting to directly discuss their own personal or private lives or that of others.

General situations can be used as examples but names and identifying descriptions should be omitted.

Distance the learning

Students should be actively discouraged from drawing on personal examples. Care should also be taken to discuss activities using the third person where possible in order to protect vulnerable individuals. Useful distancing techniques you might employ include the use of puppets, case studies or role plays with invented characters. These can be a good way to depersonalize learning so long as you take care to ensure that none of the characters in any way resembles any of your students.

Keep the conversation in the room

Students need to feel safe discussing general issues related to mental health within the lesson without fear that these discussions will be repeated by teachers or students beyond this setting. Students should feel confident exploring their misconceptions or questions about mental health within this safe setting. It is important, however, to make it clear that if you become concerned that a child may be at risk then you will need to follow the school's safeguarding policy.

Maintain a non-judgemental approach

When we tackle issues surrounding self-harm and eating disorders, we often find that students have a lot of prior beliefs, misunderstandings and inappropriate attitudes towards the topics concerned. It's important that these can be explored within the classroom environment without fear of being judged or ridiculed. Discuss with students the idea that it is okay, and often healthy, to disagree with another person's point of view but it is never okay to judge, make fun of or put down other students. Where students disagree with another's point of view, they should challenge the belief and not the person.

Ensure the right to pass

Whilst participation in the lesson is important, every student has the right to choose not to answer a question, or not to participate in an activity. Students may choose to pass on participation if a topic touches upon personal issues which they should not disclose within a classroom setting, or if the topic of the activity or discussion makes them feel uncomfortable in any way. They could be invited to discuss such concerns with the teacher individually. Teachers can prepare the class by letting them know the nature of the topic beforehand and offering students the opportunity to let the teacher know either anonymously or directly if they have any concerns about themselves or a friend. This will enable you to ensure that your teaching is as inclusive as possible and is matched to the students' needs.

If you are aware of students in your class who are likely to find the topic of the lesson particularly sensitive, perhaps due to their own pre-existing mental health condition, or that of a family member, then the lesson content could be discussed with them beforehand. It may be appropriate to give the student the right to withdraw from the lesson. They should not be expected to justify their absence to their peers. If the lesson is missed, then consideration should be taken as to how to follow up the missed lesson with the student in question so that they are able to benefit from the learning without being made to feel uncomfortable in front of their peers.

Make no assumptions

In addition to not judging the viewpoints of others, students must also take care not to make assumptions about the values, attitudes, life experiences, faith values, cultural values or feelings of their peers.

Listen to others

Every student in the class has the right to feel listened to and they should respect the right of their peers to feel listened to as well. You might choose to revisit what active listening to others means. It is okay to challenge the viewpoint of another student, but we should always listen to their point of view, in full, before making assumptions or formulating a response.

Use language carefully

Students should be reminded to take care in their use of language within (and beyond) lessons about mental health. They should not be using language that is inaccurate or offensive. There are many words surrounding mental health which have negative connotations or may be misunderstood by students. It can be valuable to explore these words and understand exactly why they are inappropriate and should not be used either within the setting of a lesson, or within day-to-day life. You might, for example, consider with students how they would feel if such words were applied to them. Such words include 'nutter' and 'loony bin' or the use of 'mental' or 'crazy' in a derogatory fashion.

Ask questions

It is important to foster an open environment where students feel safe asking questions and exploring their preconceptions about a topic. Students should understand that no question will be considered stupid and, when they are in doubt about an issue or topic, they should ask. It's also important that students realize it is never appropriate to ask a question in order to deliberately try to embarrass somebody else or to encourage students to laugh at someone.

Making an anonymous question box available to students can be an effective way of enabling students to ask questions they may feel uncomfortable posing in a classroom setting. You can make this available prior to, during or after the lesson. You will need to allow yourself time to go through and filter the questions. Inviting questions prior to the lesson can be a good way to help you direct the lesson as it progresses based on the current needs and understanding of your class and can also give a good indicator of where there are safeguarding issues or pastoral issues that are in need of follow up.

Encourage seeking help and advice

Whilst it's important that students do not make personal disclosures during the course of the lesson, the appropriate means for seeking support and advice needs to be clearly signposted in the lesson. This will mean being familiar with, and sharing appropriate parts of, the school's safeguarding policies, or other relevant policies. You should also share details of relevant websites and helplines where students can seek confidential advice and support. Students should be encouraged to support their friends in seeking help where they think it is needed. Whilst clarifying that during a lesson is not the appropriate moment to seek support, ensure students understand the importance of sharing their worries with a trusted adult if they have any concerns over their own mental health or emotional wellbeing, or that of another student. This is the quickest and best way to ensure that support is received when it is needed. Students should be reassured that they will always be taken seriously, will never be judged and will always be listened to if they choose to make a disclosure at school.

As lessons on mental health may result in students having questions they need to explore with you outside the class setting, where possible it's helpful to remain available to students immediately after class, or signpost a time when you might be available for further discussion.

TEACHING CHECKLIST

1. Familiarize yourself with school policies

Before you teach a lesson about self-harm or eating disorders, make sure you have a good understanding of your school or college's child protection policies or procedures so you know what to do if a child makes a disclosure during or following the lesson.

2. Consider vulnerable students

Even if you are unaware of any current issues amongst the students in the class you'll be teaching, prepare the lesson on the basis that there is at least one student who will be affected by the lesson content. Think carefully about how to make the lesson safe for that student – this will help to ensure it is safe for everyone.

3. Think about ground rules

You may already have well-established ground rules for teaching sensitive topics. If so, revisit them and consider which ones need re-emphasizing for today's lesson. If you don't have existing ground rules then a good start to your lesson can be to work with your students to develop a code of practice for this and similar lessons.

4. Consider likely questions/misconceptions

Help yourself to be as prepared as possible for unexpected questions by thinking through the types of questions students might come up with and thinking about how you might best answer them. Think about rumours you've heard going around school or recent headlines which might prompt discussions. There will always be questions you can't answer – and it's fine to say you'll answer them next time – but the more you can think through possible scenarios that will arise during the lesson, the more confident you'll feel teaching the topic.

5. Give students the chance to submit questions

Setting up an 'ask it basket' or anonymous question box ahead of the lesson can give students the chance to raise any questions or issues they'd like discussed in the lesson. This can be a great way for you to ensure that the lesson is shaped by students' interests and needs and can minimize the number of difficult questions you receive during the course of the lesson. This system can also prompt any vulnerable students to ask you to discuss any issues which are causing them particular distress or concern.

'I put a note in the box for the teacher asking her to discuss the fact that self-harm and suicide were very different because I knew this was something my friends didn't understand and it was a big barrier to me being able to talk to them about my problems.'

6. Distance the learning

Protect vulnerable individuals by depersonalizing learning using puppets, case studies or role plays.

7. Locate sources of school, local and national support

A key outcome of your lesson can be to ensure that students leave with the knowledge they need to seek further information and support for personal concerns or worries they may have about a friend. In order to provide the best and most relevant advice you'll need to do a little homework to ascertain what support is available at school and how it's accessed and to locate local sources of support. Often there are charities or support groups that function in the local area but may not be available nationally. Additionally, you can highlight helplines, websites and forums – these can often be a good entry point for students preparing to share their difficulties with a trusted adult but who first require the anonymity and confidentiality that is offered by many helplines and online support forums. These services will often offer sound advice and guidance to concerned friends too.

8. Tell relevant staff you'll be covering this topic

Before you teach a lesson about self-harm or eating disorders, make sure you alert other members of staff, as your lesson is very likely to trigger disclosures and staff need to know how to respond supportively and act in line with the school's policies and procedures. Holding a brief training session for staff about how to handle disclosures is an excellent idea ahead of teaching this type of lesson, if time and budget will allow. It can also be helpful to communicate with parents so that they are in a position to offer any support needed to their child.

9. Review lesson content to 'first do no harm'

Once you've prepared your lesson plan, review your material critically and consider whether any of it is likely to be triggering or upsetting for any member of the class. Remember that your key aims are to support students in developing the skills, knowledge, confidence and language they need to keep themselves and their friends safe.

Ending the lesson

It is worth considering how best to finish a lesson of this nature, which can be emotionally exhausting for both students and teacher. Students need to leave the lesson ready to continue with a busy school day. Giving students the opportunity to reflect on their learning and revisit the learning outcomes can prove reassuring as long as it is not rushed. It's also important to ensure that you reinforce messages about where and how to seek support if needed. Building in a brief more light-hearted activity at the very end of the lesson can be a good way to change the class atmosphere so that students are ready for their next lesson. Where timetabling allows, teaching this type of lesson immediately before a break/recess can work very well, and enables the teacher to remain behind to discuss any immediate concerns brought forward by individuals.

LEARNING TO TAKE AWAY FROM THIS CHAPTER

- Teaching students about self-harm and eating disorders can help to raise awareness and improve understanding, and can be used as an opportunity to highlight sources of support.

- Teaching about self-harm and eating disorders is likely to result in more students coming forward about their concerns. Staff need to be prepared to handle these disclosures.

- It is important to agree and implement ground rules when teaching about these topics in order to keep students safe.

THINGS TO DO

- Incorporate teaching about self-harm and eating disorders into your curriculum.

- Identify sources of school, local and national support for self-harm and eating disorders and signpost these for students.

- Follow the teaching checklist at the end of this chapter when preparing lessons which feature self-harm or eating disorders.

CHAPTER 4

Why Students Develop Unhealthy Coping Mechanisms

This chapter will enable you to:

- explore the common misconceptions that people have about why students develop unhealthy coping mechanisms like self-harm and eating disorders

- understand a range of reasons why students might develop unhealthy coping behaviours

- respond appropriately to a student who claims to be self-harming when in fact he is not.

Common misconceptions about why people self-harm

Two of the most common misconceptions about students who self-harm are that all students who self-harm are attention seeking and that all students who self-harm are feeling suicidal.

These opposing viewpoints can cause people to either dismiss self-harming behaviour or over-react in response to it. Both responses are stigmatizing and unhelpful to sufferers, making them less likely to seek support for their self-harming behaviour.

The belief that all self-harming behaviour is attention seeking arises from the fact that some students who are carrying out relatively superficial self-harming activity actively display their injuries or share images of their self-harm online with friends.

'She was walking round school with her sleeves rolled up showing off these tiny scratches on her arms. It was a transparent attempt at attention seeking.'

'It's just what students do these days. They used to dye their hair or pierce their nose but now if they want our attention they burn holes in their arms.'

It's important that we don't dismiss these students as 'attention seeking' – clearly they are trying to convey a message of some kind and, rather than dismissing their behaviour, we should ask ourselves what message they are trying to convey. Why are they in need of support and can we help? I like to think of these students as 'seeking attention' rather than attention seeking. They may be using their injuries to indicate that they are in need of help and support because they don't know how else to communicate their concerns.

Another counter-argument to the belief that all students who self-harm are attention seeking is the fact that so many cases of self-harm go undetected. For many students, self-harming is a behaviour of which they feel ashamed and so it is carried out completely in secret. Many students go to great lengths to hide their injuries, wearing long sleeves in warm weather, avoiding changing in front of others, or harming parts of the body which are easier to hide such as the top of their thigh or their stomach. Many students who self-harm go undetected for months or years; some of them will never become known to us.

> 'I was very careful and calculating about it. I knew that cuts at the top of my legs would be easier to hide. I became a master at skiving out of PE and swimming and I never went clothes shopping with friends so they wouldn't see my legs. I went to great lengths to make sure no one found out. Nobody would ever have known if I hadn't owned up and asked for help.'

Whilst many people dismiss self-harming behaviour as meaningless and attention seeking, other people assume that all acts of self-harm are driven by a student's desire to end their life. This assumption is particularly often made when students take non-lethal overdoses or cut their arms. As discussed in Chapter 1, suicidal ideation is not the over-riding reason behind most instances of self-harm and the majority of students who self-harm have never felt suicidal. Over-dramatizing self-harm acts by believing them to be suicidal can be very damaging to students, who end up feeling misunderstood and unable to share their real motives and concerns.

> 'The first time, I took the tablets on a whim. I didn't want to die, I just wanted everything to go numb for a little while but then I panicked and told my mum. No one would believe that I didn't want to die. They treated me like a total head case and just wouldn't listen to me. I felt like no one could understand what was really going on. After that I took tablets again quite a few times but I never made the mistake of telling anyone.'

Common misconceptions about why people develop eating disorders

There are also a number of common misconceptions about the reasons people develop eating disorders, with many people dismissing them as sheer vanity, diets which should not be a cause for concern or a passing phase which will be grown out of.

The idea that eating disorders are a disease of vanity is borne out of our obsession with the pursuit of thinness and the ideals of beauty we see within the media. It's true that the pressure to be slim and beautiful may impact on some students, and we need to encourage self-esteem and body confidence at all sizes, but the reality is that an eating disorder is an enduring psychological illness which drives the sufferer to extreme behaviours which simply would not be sustainable simply in the pursuit of vanity. In addition to this, as we'll explore later in this chapter, many people suffering with eating disorders are actively hoping to make themselves appear unattractive.

Eating disorders are dismissed by some as diets, or passing phases which should not be a cause for concern and which are likely to correct themselves without intervention. Whilst this may be true for students experimenting with dieting, for those who have developed or are well on the road to developing a full-blown eating disorder, this simply is not the case. Eating disorders are serious mental health issues and, in many cases, the student affected is unlikely to recover without either focused support, professional treatment or a significant change in their underlying circumstances.

Why do students develop self-harm and eating disorders?

There are a wide range of reasons why people develop unhealthy coping mechanisms such as self-harm and eating disorders. Every single case is different but, when I talk to students about the reasons underlying their issues, there are certain themes that recur time and time again.

In the following pages I have shared some quotes and case studies from students who have been brave enough to share their stories with me to illustrate some of the most common reasons students cite for developing unhealthy coping mechanisms. Each case study is accompanied by a few questions – these are designed to get you thinking but could also be used alongside the case studies as part of a training session with colleagues or parents to help to raise awareness and increase understanding. It is not recommended that you use the full case studies with students as they provide too much detailed information about the mechanisms underlying the eating disorders and self-harm, so they may exacerbate issues being experienced by vulnerable students in your care.

Control

During adolescence, a time when students are keen to assert their independence, they can begin to feel very out of control of their own lives. This can be for a number of reasons: perhaps their life is in chaos with difficult relationships at home or school, or perhaps they feel like they're being told what to do every minute of the day and don't have the freedom they'd like from parents or teachers. When you can't control anything else in your life, you can completely control your own body and your food intake.

> 'I know it's a really negative kind of control but when your whole life is complete s**t you take what you can, y'know? And as I burnt myself I would feel in control for a while. I guess I was on self-destruct and that was bad but at least it was me holding the flame.'

> 'The day I realized that nobody could take control of my body but me, I felt really powerful. In the past I'd been weak and other people had controlled my body but now it's mine. I can care for it if I want to care for it and I can hurt it if I want to hurt it. It's *mine*.'

> 'I'm 16. Every day of my life I've been told what to do from the moment I wake up to the moment I go to sleep. I'm sick of it. This is just my secret way of having a bit of control in my life.'

Similarly, it is very common for a student with an eating disorder to believe that food is the only part of their life that they can exert any control over. Ironically, when they feel most in control, that is, restricting their food intake very heavily, is when they are in fact most out of control and unable to break the cycle of the illness.

The case study below illustrates how 14-year-old Rae felt that her eating disorder gave her more control in her life. It is followed by a few questions to help you think about how Rae was feeling and what motivated her to continue to restrict her food intake. You might find these questions useful to explore with colleagues.

Case study: Rae, 14, anorexia nervosa

Rae was 12 when her eating disorder was diagnosed. She'd been going through a difficult time at home; her elderly grandmother had recently moved in with the family which had caused disputes between her parents and put pressure on Rae who was expected to help with her grandmother's care. Rae's friends had started meeting up in town after school but Rae felt unable to join them as she had too much homework and responsibility to her grandmother. She began to feel increasingly ignored, unimportant and out of control of her own life. Her weight loss started almost by accident. She'd eaten very sporadically for a few days as she'd been so busy at home and school and she was surprised, and pleased, to see that she had lost a couple of pounds when she weighed herself. She wondered what she would need to do to lose more weight and started to think up a few dieting rules for herself.

Over the next few weeks, Rae added more dieting and exercise rules into her daily routine. She took great pleasure in seeing the impact that her dieting and exercising was having on her weight and felt, for once, like there was one aspect of her life over which she had complete control.

Sadly, Rae's grandmother passed away within a few months. Rae had grown very close to her and was hit hard by her loss, despite its inevitability. Once again, Rae felt out of control of her life and her emotions and she found that placing more emphasis on her diet and exercise rules gave her something to think about that was less painful than mourning her grandmother and which gave her a real sense of achievement. Soon Rae's whole life was dominated by rules she had developed regarding food and exercise. She carefully noted her daily allowance and schedule in a special notebook and prioritized her food and exercise rules above everything else in her life.

Questions to consider

1. What was making Rae feel out of control? Can you imagine students in your care sharing these feelings?

2. Why did Rae feel more in control when she introduced rules around diet and exercise? What motivated her to continue?

3. When Rae's personal situation worsened, she responded by introducing further controls of her diet and exercise. In what ways do you think this would have been helpful and/or unhelpful to her whilst mourning the loss of her grandmother?

4. It sounds like Rae was very much in control of her food intake – was she?

5. How do you think Rae felt when she didn't adhere to her rules? How do you think she might have responded?

Punishment

Some people talk about using self-harm as a way of punishing themselves when they don't live up to expectations – this tends to either be students who are perfectionist in nature, or those with a history of systematic abuse who have learned that they 'deserve' to be punished.

> 'If I didn't do as well as I'd hoped, I'd take a load of pills and go to sleep. It made me numb. Kind of like a mini coma. It was the only way I could stop thinking about how I'd let myself down.'

> 'I was always punished as a kid. If I was late, if I did something stupid, if I didn't do well enough at school. My Dad used to hit me to teach me a lesson. Once I went into care I guess I kind of took over the punishment myself. People would tell me that it was okay to make mistakes and I shouldn't punish myself but it made me feel better.'

Students with eating disorders sometimes refer to punishing themselves too, saying that they don't think they deserve to eat. Depriving themselves of food could be considered a form of self-harm in this instance.

> 'I hated myself so much and constantly felt a need to be punished for not being perfect at school, for being a bad daughter, for not being popular enough. I used to love food so depriving myself of it felt like a good punishment.'

And some students talk about wanting to disappear because they feel they don't deserve to be alive:

> 'Every time I lost another pound, I felt like I was a step closer to disappearing completely. I didn't deserve to exist but I wasn't brave enough to kill myself. It was like a very gradual suicide.'

To appear ugly

Some students specifically talk about wanting to punish themselves by making themselves appear ugly. This kind of response is sometimes seen in students who have suffered the trauma of abuse or rape. Some students feel responsible for the abuse they've suffered and try to punish themselves by making themselves less desirable.

> 'When I thought back to that night, I realized I was 'asking for it'. I thought I looked good and I guess I was flaunting myself a bit. I guess I made him want me too much. Afterwards I was so ashamed and disgusted at myself. I repeatedly burned my breasts with acid. I wanted to make them as ugly as possible so I wouldn't want to flaunt them any more.'

For some students, the idea of becoming ugly can also feel like a protective factor against future abuse:

> 'I took a weird pleasure in burning my body with cigarettes. I never burned anywhere that showed but if someone were to try and take my clothes off they would see the repulsive weeping wounds all over my body. If a man tried to run his hand up my thigh again he would feel the ragged edges of my oozing sores. I'm sure it would repulse him and he would go and pick on someone else.'

Some students talk about making themselves less sexually attractive through starvation:

> 'I was raped and it scared me so much. I didn't ever tell anyone but I made the decision that I didn't want a man to ever want me like that again. Now I'm ugly and thin, no one will want me and I won't get hurt.'

> 'I don't really look like a woman any more. As I got thinner I lost my hips and my boobs went away. Boys don't fancy me and I like it that way. I feel safer.'

To manage overwhelming feelings

For people who struggle to communicate or express their feelings in another way, self-harming or disordered eating behaviours can feel like the only way to communicate and release those feelings.

> 'I'm not good with words. I'm good at cutting. When there are more cuts it means I need more help.'

> 'Sometimes I'd have so many different feelings inside me I thought I was going to explode. Then I'd cut myself and I'd instantly feel a bit better, the feelings flowed away down the plughole as I washed the blood away.'

Food is frequently used as a way of responding to difficult emotions. Some people feed those emotions whilst others try to starve them away:

> 'The more I ate, the more the pain would numb. It was temporary – like a drug high – but I craved those few moments in my day when everything felt okay.'

> 'As I got thinner my brain slowed down. After a few months, the old thoughts that used to torment me were barely there. As I starved my brain it became incapable of tormenting me. It was wonderful at first.'

For some people, physical pain can be a way of communicating emotional pain which is too hard to talk about. For some, it can provide a more manageable form of pain that they can tend to rather than facing up to the emotional and psychological injuries they may be suffering with, for example, as a result of abuse.

'I was right messed up and I didn't know how to make it go away, but some days I felt like maybe I could physically cut away the pain.'

'It was a physical expression of the emotional pain I was feeling but couldn't begin to explain.'

'Cutting was something I could talk about and ask for support with unlike the other things that were going on.'

Case study: Jamal, 16, cutting

Jamal was taken into care at the age of six when he was removed from his parents who were charged with neglect and abuse. He has always refused to talk about his early years though he has seen a number of therapists who found him to be quiet and unassuming and not presenting any specific cause for concern. Jamal eventually settled in a foster home at the age of 14, having been moved between different care homes for many years. Eighteen months into his placement, it was felt that Jamal had really landed on his feet. He appeared to have really bonded with his foster parents and had struck up a good relationship with a second foster child living with the family, but he still never talked about his early years.

But things soon began to change. Jamal started to truant school and was having trouble sleeping and started to become quick to upset and anger. He began cutting his arms – something he made no attempt to hide and which he would always tell his foster mum about straight away, asking for her help in cleaning and dressing the wounds. As she cleaned the wounds, Jamal would openly weep – showing his emotions in a way he had not been known to do before, but still he did not talk about his early years and the reasons underlying his cutting.

Questions to consider

1. Why do you think Jamal never talked about his early years?

2. Why do you suppose Jamal started to self-harm just as it seemed he was finally more settled and happy?

3. Do you think it was significant that Jamal asked his foster mum for help with his wounds each time he cut? What messages do his actions convey?

4. Why did Jamal cry as his foster mother helped to clean his wounds?

5. Do you think Jamal's self-harming showed a step forwards or backwards in his recovery from his early abuse?

Nowhere else to turn

Some students describe not being aware of a better way to deal with their problems as being a key motivation behind self-harming and disordered eating behaviours.

'Some people drink, some people take drugs, some people paint pictures, I burn myself. It's not really that big a deal, it's just the way I deal with things.'

'Eating's the only thing that makes me feel better. Nothing else I've tried gets through.'

To feel pure or clean

'I like to feel empty, it makes me feel clean and pure inside. The best kind of empty is when you haven't eaten or drunk anything but I always find that too hard, so I make myself sick after I've eaten and keep on throwing up until I feel empty again. Then I feel better.'

This is a fairly commonly expressed viewpoint, though this tends to be more of a reason why an eating disorder is maintained rather than why it starts in the first place. An exception to this is students who have found starving for religious reasons such as Ramadan to feel physically, emotionally and spiritually rewarding. This has been reported to act as a trigger for disordered eating in some students.

To feel cared for

For a minority of students who self-harm, the motivation is not in the self-harming incident itself, but the aftercare. In particular, students who have suffered from neglect in the past may find the care that is administered to them, or which they can administer to themselves, following a self-harming incident to be very rewarding.

'As the nurse cleaned my wounds, I felt looked after and cared for in a way that I just wasn't used to. I liked it so I did it again.'

'I guess I felt no one was ever going to care for me so I needed to care for myself. The more badly I burned myself the more care I could give myself. I developed a weird fascination with the different creams and bandages I could buy. It became a real ritual for me.'

Similarly, some people observe the support received by others in response to their self-harm and realize that harming may be a way of accessing similar help and support for themselves; this can be especially true if they don't know how else to ask for help for underlying issues they feel unable to talk about.

'It sounds pretty dumb when I talk about it now, but I remember at the time being really envious of all the attention my friend was getting for her self-harming. She would cut her arms and people would make time for her, care for her, check in on her and make sure she was okay. I guess I just felt like I needed similar support because of everything that was going on at home, but I didn't know how to ask. So I copied her and started cutting too. It worked and I got the help I needed.'

Responding to invented or imagined self-harm

Recently I've increasingly been asked how to respond to students who are confiding in friends, teachers or parents about self-harm or eating-disordered behaviour that isn't actually happening. Relatively frequently, I am told about students who are circulating pictures of their self-harm via social media or mobile messaging, but that when a concerned friend raises the issue with a trusted adult, the self-harm turns out to be images of a stranger's self-harm sourced online. Similarly some students may talk openly about how they are severely restricting their food intake, but this turns out to be untrue.

In these instances you can't help but wonder why someone would invent these kinds of issues. Every case is different and there are a wide range of reasons that students would fabricate self-harm but the most obvious reason would be as a cry for help and an attempt to access support.

The case of 13-year-old Rowena is fairly typical:

Case study: Rowena, 13, invented self-harm

Rowena was new to her school. Due to a change in her father's employment situation, the family had moved to a new town in the middle of the school year. Rowena had seemed quiet and withdrawn since starting the school a few weeks ago and recently came to the attention of the school staff after a concerned friend talked to a teacher, confiding that Rowena had been sharing images on Facebook and Instagram of burns on her arms and legs. The school has been made aware that Rowena's older brother had self-harmed in the past.

In line with the school policy, a teacher sat down with Rowena to understand what was happening and how the school might best support her. However, when the teacher spoke to Rowena and suggested that her mother would need to be informed about her self-harming, Rowena admitted that the images she'd shared online were not of her own arms and legs. She rolled up her trouser legs and shirt sleeves to reveal no injuries. Rowena was deeply distraught and through her tears could not even begin to explain why she had pretended to be self-harming.

Questions to consider

1. What do you think Rowena hoped would happen after she shared images online?

2. How might the fact her brother has self-harmed in the past have impacted on Rowena's decision to pretend she was burning herself?

3. How would you respond?

4. Would it be appropriate to reprimand Rowena or dismiss her concerns? Why/why not?

Rowena had recently moved to a new town and new school in the middle of the school year. Like any child who moves mid-year and who is transplanted away from their friendship group, she was likely to go through a difficult period of transition. She may not have known who or how to ask for the support that she needed whilst making new friends and establishing a new support network. But by inventing a story that gained people's sympathy she probably hoped to receive a response that she would feel very comforted by and which would help her during the period of transition. She may have considered a supportive response especially likely as her brother had previously self-harmed and she may have noted the support and care he was given in response to his behaviours and injuries in the past.

Students sharing images of other people's self-harm and passing them off as their own is something that I hear of relatively frequently in schools where there are several students who are known to have self-harmed and who've received good support from the school and/or peers. Self-harming is suddenly seen, by some, as a good way to receive support and attention. Sharing images of other people's self-harm may be perceived to achieve the same outcome but without the actual harm taking place.

So should we continue to support someone like Rowena once it becomes apparent that the problem they're seeking help for is fabricated? My answer is an unequivocal YES. In order for a student to go to the lengths of inventing a scenario for which they might receive some support, there must be some underlying issues or difficulties for which they genuinely do need support. They may be unable or unwilling to communicate the underlying issues which might be why they've chosen to express their worries in a different way.

How can we best help?

Try not to be angry with the student for lying – this will make them feel ashamed and embarrassed and far less likely to open up to you or someone else about what the underlying problem is. It may also make them far more likely to carry out actual self-harm as they may perceive that their attempt at help seeking has failed purely because their injuries were fabricated. Instead give them your time and undivided attention and listen. Let them know that you're happy to support them and do not obsess over why they felt the need to invent stories. Focus on building a trusting relationship so that you can help them work through any underlying issues. This same approach can be applied to those students whose injuries or eating behaviours are relatively low level but where emotional distress is clearly quite high.

LEARNING TO TAKE AWAY FROM THIS CHAPTER

- Commonly held misconceptions about why students develop unhealthy coping mechanisms can be stigmatizing and prevent them seeking the support they need.

- There are a wide range of reasons that students cite for their unhealthy behaviours. Taking steps towards understanding these reasons can help us to make sense of behaviours which might seem alien otherwise.

- Students who pretend they are self-harming or restricting their food intake need to be treated sensitively and listened to, otherwise there is a risk they will actually carry out these behaviours.

THINGS TO DO

- Challenge misconceptions about self-harm and eating disorders when you hear them.

- Educate colleagues about some of the reasons underlying self-harming and eating-disordered behaviours by using the case studies and questions shared in this chapter.

CHAPTER 5

Factors that Put Students at Risk of Eating Disorders and Self-Harm

This chapter will enable you to:

- understand the personality, family and social factors that put some students more at risk of developing unhealthy coping mechanisms than others

- consider the protective factors that may aid a student's resilience and ability to overcome their difficulties

- understand common triggers that often mark the onset of a student's difficulties.

Whilst self-harm and eating disorders can affect anyone, some students are more at risk than others and are worth keeping a closer eye on. This chapter outlines a wide range of risk factors. Not all students with the risk factors outlined will go on to develop self-harming or eating-disordered behaviours and, equally, some students will go on to develop unhealthy coping mechanisms without ever apparently meeting any of the risk criteria outlined over the next few pages. However, an awareness of these risk factors can help you to identify the more vulnerable children in your care so that you can be extra vigilant for early symptoms of self-harm and eating disorders.

Personality risk factors

There are a range of personality factors that can put a student at higher risk than their peers of developing self-harming or eating-disordered behaviours. These are all characteristics and traits that are directly observable once you get to know a child and many of them are very evident within the school environment, even if they are not evident at home.

Difficulty expressing feelings and emotions

Students who are unable to express their feelings or emotions very well may turn to food as a way of expressing themselves. This might not make immediate sense to you – but think about how often we console ourselves with a chocolate bar, an ice cream or a packet of crisps when we're feeling down about something. Eating disorder sufferers take this quite normal behaviour to a whole new level, using food to help them control and express their emotions.

Some students will turn to self-harm as well/instead. Students who are struggling to deal with extreme feelings of sadness, anger or frustration often talk about the immense relief that the act of self-harming can bring. There are a range of different reasons why a student may have difficulty expressing their feelings and emotions. It may be that they just aren't a natural communicator, it may be that they have special or additional educational needs or a disability (such as a hearing impairment) which makes it more difficult for them to communicate, or it might be that they have not developed the skills and language they need to effectively communicate their thoughts and feelings. This can be especially true of younger children who may turn readily to self-harming or unusual eating behaviours to manage or express extreme emotions. Children who are not communicating in their first language in the school environment can also be more vulnerable for this reason as they may not have the language skills they need to communicate their concerns to friends or trusted adults at school.

> 'I couldn't talk about it. I didn't have the right words and I didn't think anyone would want to listen. I felt better when I cut. It was like I could just cut all the anger out of me.'

A tendency to comply with others' demands

Well-behaved children with a real respect for rules are more at risk of suffering from eating disorders than their peers. Many eating disorders are bound up in a series of complex rules with sufferers creating special guidelines for themselves about their diet and exercise. For example, a student with anorexia might have a strict rule about the number of calories they're allowed to eat in a day or a bulimic might force themselves to be sick a specific number of times after eating a particular type of food.

Very high expectations of achievement

Students who have a perfectionist personality type, are very hard on themselves and aim high with their academic work are more likely to apply this type of approach to food and dieting, either pushing themselves to achieve a lower and lower weight, or to do increasing amounts of exercise. They are also more likely than most students to give themselves a hard time when they don't meet their own exacting standards either in their academic or personal life. They may use food to help them cope or to punish themselves.

These students can also go through their day-to-day lives feeling a constant fear of failure. The standards they set for themselves tend to be unrealistic or unsustainable and what may be considered excellence by most children may be seen as failure by the perfectionist child. When they fail to meet the very high standards they set themselves, these students may punish themselves in a variety of ways, such as restricting their food intake or carrying out self-harming behaviours such as cutting or burning.

> 'Everyone said I was doing really well, but it was never good enough for me. I always wanted more, to do the very best. But it was hard. I put so much pressure on myself to achieve what I maybe wasn't even capable of, that in the end I broke and started bingeing and cutting in order to cope with the pressure.'

> 'I was your typical high achiever. All set for medical school. The works. I found at some point that I got great pleasure from taking control of my diet and weight. Of course, I had to be the best at that as well so I would be following a very strict study timetable on the one hand and an even stricter diet plan on the other.'

Low mood/anxiety and low self-esteem

It's common for students to suffer with self-harm or eating disorders alongside other mental health issues, most notably anxiety or depression. Students who have been diagnosed with one of these conditions should be specifically monitored for signs of other unhealthy coping mechanisms. In addition to those with specific diagnoses, it is worth paying careful attention to students who are more prone than their peers to general signs of low mood or anxious behaviours.

Similarly, low self-esteem is also associated with self-harm and all forms of eating disorders. Coping with the negative feelings associated with low self-esteem can increase the likelihood of students needing to develop day-to-day coping mechanisms, and their lack of self-worth can lead them to be less ready to dismiss self-abusive behaviours than more confident peers who may recognize that it is inappropriate to treat themselves so badly.

> 'When my mum found out, the thing she couldn't get her head round was why I thought it was okay to treat my body this way. I couldn't understand why she thought I deserved anything better.'

Poor problem-solving skills

Students who have poor problem-solving skills are more likely than their peers to turn to behaviours such as self-harm and eating disorders. Peers with better problem-solving skills may be better able to develop more healthy coping mechanisms or seek appropriate help and support. Some children with special or additional educational needs tend to have worse than average problem-solving skills.

> 'I just wanted to make my problems go away. Drinking did that.'

Impulsivity or drug and alcohol use

Students who are more impulsive are more likely than their peers to develop self-harming behaviours. Carrying out a self-harm act for the first time is quite a leap from normal behaviour and is more likely to be carried out by students who are more impulsive or whose inhibitions have been lowered through, for example, drug or alcohol use.

> 'The first time I cut myself I was wasted…once I'd done it once, doing it again seemed like less of a big deal.'

Family life risk factors

Supportive families are the most helpful resource a student can draw on in their recovery. Family life should not be seen as the cause of self-harm or eating disorders in any but the most extreme circumstances (e.g. if there is neglect or abuse at home). However, there are some types of home environment that can contribute to the possibility of a vulnerable student developing unhealthy coping mechanisms.

Unreasonably high academic expectations

If a family consistently places academic expectations upon a student which are unrealistically high or unsustainable, then this pressure can lead to the development of issues such as a self-harm and eating disorders. This can commonly occur when a younger sibling is less able either academically or physically than an older sibling to whose standards they are expected to aspire.

> 'I spent my whole time trying, and failing, to be as good as my older brother.'

It's worth noting that these expectations are often perceived rather than actual. Students often think that their parents have certain expectations of them or that they are expected to follow in the footsteps of a successful older sibling when this pressure is, in fact, coming from the student rather than from their parents.

Controlling or protective family

One of the reasons that students often cite for developing self-harm and eating-disordered behaviours is a desire for control within their lives, therefore it stands to reason that students living in families where they are afforded very little control are more at risk than their peers of developing these issues.

> 'Every minute of my day was scripted by my mum, by my teacher, by my coach. I couldn't control anything…except what I ate.'

This type of environment is often created with the best interests of the child very much in mind, in a bid to keep them safe or enable them to succeed academically. However, students who feel that they do not have a significant say in their own life may struggle. This can be especially hard for students whose families are stricter or more protective than their friends' families, perhaps meaning that their friends are allowed to go out together but the student in question is not allowed to join in.

Some families can become more overprotective of a child in response to trauma such as the loss or illness of a child within the family. In these circumstances it is entirely understandable that parents may want to do everything in their power to keep their children safe but it can have the consequence of making a child feel smothered and lacking in autonomy.

Cultural identity conflict

A student who feels out of place amongst their peers can be at higher risk of developing unhealthy coping mechanisms. The majority of students want nothing more than to be 'normal' and many can feel that they are unlike their friends due to cultural differences. A student whose family have moved to the country from abroad can sometimes end up feeling that they don't quite fit with their peers, but nor do they really fit amongst their family and this feeling of being an unhappy hybrid can be a risk factor for unhealthy coping mechanisms. Equally, children from families who have strong beliefs, religious or otherwise, which set the child apart from their peers can experience a feeling of not belonging.

> 'I didn't know who I was. I felt confused and conflicted all the time and just couldn't cope.'

Children in care
Students who are currently, or have previously been, in the care system, are more at risk of self-harm and eating disorders. This is both because many students in care have suffered either abuse or neglect and that all of them must process the fact of being separated from their birth family, which can lead to questions around identity, belonging and feeling loved or wanted.

Young carer's role
Students who contribute to the care of a loved one at home, either due to illness or due to parental absence, are at elevated risk of turning to unhealthy coping mechanisms. The reasons for this are twofold. First, caring for a loved one is a huge responsibility and can cause the student to feel quite stressed or under pressure. Second, the student in question is unlikely to confide in their family if they feel in need of support. They will often feel that they do not want to cause further concern to their family or that their concerns are trivial. Therefore, rather than discussing their issues, they are more likely to turn to mechanisms they can use to cope with their problems without sharing them.

> 'My sister had been dying for as long as I could remember. It was very sad and very stressful. I didn't really feel like I could talk to anyone about my problems, they seemed so small, so I just found my own ways of coping.'

Neglect or any form of abuse
Children who have suffered from neglect or abuse are very vulnerable to a wide range of mental health and emotional wellbeing issues. This is in part due to the stress and trauma they have suffered, and in part due to the fact that their abuse or neglect may have incorrectly taught them

that they are worthless or deserve to be punished. This has the result of making self-harming behaviours feel like less inappropriate acts than they might feel to another child who had not suffered in the same way.

> 'I have always been hated. My mum hated me for years. Once I was taken away from her I started hating myself, and punishing myself.'

Poor relationships with parents

For many students, their parents are the most trusted adults in their lives and an important source of advice and support. Where this relationship is absent or not as positive as it might be, this can leave a gap in a student's support network and make them more vulnerable to internalizing and inappropriately responding to emotional difficulties.

Social life risk factors

There are a range of external influences such as hobbies and friendships which can impact on a student's risk of developing self-harm and eating disorders.

Confusion about sexuality or gender

Students who experience any form of uncertainty about their sexuality or their gender are at heightened risk of turning to unhealthy coping mechanisms, and especially self-harm, as they may be frustrated or disgusted by their own body.

> 'I was so horrified at my own body when I started to grow breasts that I cut them. I was trying to cut them away so I could turn this girl's body into the boy's body I should have had.'

Being bullied or teased

The stress and upset caused by being teased or bullied can make students very vulnerable to developing mental health or emotional wellbeing issues. Students who are bullied about their weight, shape or appearance are especially vulnerable to developing eating disorders whilst those who are bullied about their sexuality are more prone than their peers to self-harm.

Friends who have suffered from self-harm or eating disorders

Having a close friend who is suffering from an eating disorder or who is self-harming can be very stressful, both because it is upsetting to see a friend experience these difficulties and because a student may end up taking on a pseudo-counsellor role for their friend and feel frustrated, upset or angry when they can't solve the problem. This stress alone can leave a student more vulnerable to developing unhealthy coping mechanisms themselves, especially if they are not offered appropriate support. The likelihood of developing self-harming or eating-disordered behaviours can also be exacerbated if these coping mechanisms are observed to be in some way helpful to the student who is suffering, either because they openly share that the behaviours themselves are rewarding or because of the supportive response they might receive as a result of these behaviours.

> 'Every time she burnt herself, she got offered help. People listened to her, helped her, cared for her. I was really stressed and needed similar support but didn't know how to ask for it. In the end, I asked for it by cutting.'

Highly competitive hobbies

Participating in highly competitive hobbies can be extremely rewarding, however, they can place a lot of pressure on students which needs to be appropriately managed. The high stakes involved in, for instance, playing sports at county level can result in some students feeling anxious and fearing failure, which can increase the likelihood of them turning to unhealthy coping mechanisms such as self-harm and eating disorders. Additionally, some hobbies such as dance, gymnastics and boxing place specific requirements on physique, weight or fitness which can make students more vulnerable to developing eating disorders as they can become preoccupied with 'making weight'.

Additionally, activities which take up a large proportion of students' time can exacerbate the feeling of a lack of control over their own life and leave them with little down-time. This is true of students with a wide range of interests in addition to sport, including choristers and musicians, for example.

Resilience factors

Considering the factors that put a student more at risk of developing unhealthy coping mechanisms can feel like quite a bleak activity, but it's important to remember that, as well as factors that put them at risk, students all have a series of factors which help to aid their resilience and may help to protect them against the development of self-harming or eating-disordered behaviours or could be drawn upon to assist them during recovery if problems did arise.

Often, the factors that we consider to put children most at risk are the same factors which can add to their resilience when turned on their head. For example, we talked earlier in this chapter about how a protective family might put a child at risk, but the same family are likely to be very invested in, and supportive of, the recovery process. Equally, a student who is very high achieving and perfectionist in nature may be more at risk of developing an eating disorder than their peers, but if this motivation and determined attitude can be refocused then it can be a fantastic tool for recovery.

It's important to look for both risk and resilience factors when considering the students in our care to give us the best possible chance of promoting their wellbeing. This will help you to gain a more well-rounded view of any individual who might be giving you cause for concern and will help you to consider factors in their lifestyle or personality that you may be able to draw on when supporting their recovery.

Triggers

For those children more at risk of mental health and emotional wellbeing difficulties, there are a series of triggers you should be aware of which may make the student in question more likely to turn to an unhealthy mechanism such as an eating disorder or self-harm. Whilst some difficulties may develop gradually, such as food restriction or emotionally overeating, for others there is a distinct moment when the student in question crosses a line – for example, when they induce vomiting for the first time or commit their first act of self-harm. These initial acts are often a response to a specific circumstance or set of circumstances. The most common triggers described by students reflecting on when their own difficulties started are outlined below. It is worth ensuring that students in your care who experience any of these triggers are provided with specific support and care to try and prevent the onset of eating-disordered or self-harming behaviour; this is especially important if the student in question is at higher risk than their peers of developing unhealthy coping mechanisms.

Family relationship difficulties

Difficulties at home can take a huge toll on a student's emotional wellbeing. The difficulties may be between the parents or may concern the student directly – such as a difficult falling out with a parent or sibling. Stable family relationships are a fantastic source of emotional support for students, so it's important to think about where that support is coming from, and what extra support might be needed, when things are difficult at home.

Peer relationship break up/difficulties

Similarly, difficult relationships at school, whether platonic or romantic, can leave students feeling desperate and with no one to turn to. In these instances they are far more likely to turn to unhealthy coping mechanisms such as self-harm, eating disorders or substance abuse.

Bullying

Unfortunately, bullying is a feature of many students' lives, with up to one in four people being bullied by the time they leave school. This experience can be hugely damaging to a student's self-esteem and leave them struggling to cope with difficult emotions. Students who are bullied because of their weight or appearance are especially at risk.

Trauma

Experiencing trauma, for example a bereavement, being involved in an accident or suffering abuse, will leave a student very vulnerable and in huge need of support. It's important to bear in mind that this is about the student's perception of trauma, not our own. Difficulties may be triggered by something seemingly insignificant, but which has impacted deeply on the student concerned, such as the death of a pet.

Being exposed to unhealthy coping mechanisms in other students or the media

When students are exposed to self-harm, eating disorders or other unhealthy coping mechanisms either by witnessing them first hand or by watching them on TV or the internet, they are more likely to replicate those behaviours themselves. You should be especially vigilant if high-profile programmes watched by a large number of students run stories involving eating disorders or self-harm.

Difficult times of year, such as anniversaries

The anniversary of a significant event such as the death of a parent is often a very difficult time for students. Birthdays and Christmas can also be trigger points. It is sensible to keep a note of any such dates on student files as it is not uncommon for problems to arise seemingly out of the blue many years after the trauma, as a student marks a milestone anniversary or if a student is also contending with other difficulties that coincide with an anniversary, which then pushes them over the edge.

Trouble in school or with the police

If a student gets into significant trouble at school or with the police, this can be hugely stressful and can lead to them turning to coping mechanisms such as alcohol, drugs or self-harm.

Exam pressure

The pressure of exams is keenly felt by students and is a very common trigger for mental health problems. You should be keeping an extra-close eye on students as they enter periods of exams and also during times when academic pressure significantly increases – such as when they have to make important subject choices, or when they embark on examined courses.

Transition to a new school

Transition to a new school can be very difficult for students who may miss the familiarity of their old setting and may need to establish new friendship groups. This is true of students who are making the natural progression 'up to big school' even if they are accompanied by some of their friends, and is even more acute for children who move schools part way through a school year due, for instance, to a family move or following a permanent exclusion.

Illness in the family

If a parent or sibling falls seriously ill, this can put a huge pressure on a student who is likely to take on some form of caring role whilst inevitably receiving less time and attention from loved ones due to the focus on the family member who is unwell. They may also be harbouring deep worries about the wellbeing of their relative. In this situation, students often feel unable to voice their worries or concerns for fear of being a burden and may instead turn to other coping mechanisms such as alcohol, drugs or self-harm.

LEARNING TO TAKE AWAY FROM THIS CHAPTER

- There are a wide range of factors which can increase students' vulnerability to developing unhealthy coping mechanisms. Becoming familiar with these factors can help us to identify students to keep a closer eye on.

- Sometimes the same factor which increases the risk of a student developing unhealthy coping mechanisms can be turned on its head and used as a resilience factor to drive recovery.

- There are a series of common triggers which we should be aware of which may result in the onset of unhealthy coping mechanisms in some students.

THINGS TO DO

- Consider the students in your care and identify any whose personality, family or social profiles put them at higher risk than their peers of developing unhealthy coping mechanisms.

- Where possible, make a note on students' files about any potentially triggering situations or events – such as the birthday of a deceased parent. Offer extra support to students at times when common triggers increase the likelihood of self-harm or eating disorder onset.

CHAPTER 6

Early Symptoms of Eating Disorders and Self-Harm

This chapter will enable you to:

- understand the importance of early recognition of self-harm and eating disorders

- recognize the early signs and symptoms which may indicate a young person is suffering from eating-disordered or self-harming behaviours.

The importance of spotting the signs early

School staff are uniquely well placed to spot self-harm and eating disorder warning signs which may be hidden at home. Sport/physical education teachers in particular often spot the physical warning signs very early on. The earlier that symptoms are detected and treated, the better the prognosis for the student involved, as behaviours will have had less opportunity to become entrenched and the student may be more open to offers of support. Early detection can drastically reduce the degree and duration of intervention needed to ensure recovery and is far more likely to result in a full and lasting recovery.

Early warning signs to look out for

The following pages outline some of the most common warning signs that might indicate a student is developing self-harming or eating-disordered behaviours. But the most important thing you can do is to *trust your gut instinct – if you feel that a student is in need of support, then follow up on that instinct.* You'll find that you're rarely wrong once you've been working with young people for a while.

Weight change

Key indicators of eating disorders are weight loss in the case of anorexia and weight gain in the case of binge eating disorder, and we sometimes (but don't always) see weight fluctuation in students with bulimia. This weight change is often very noticeable after a school holiday and we should be just as concerned about a student who has rapidly gained a significant amount of weight as we should be about one who has lost a significant amount of weight.

Isolation

If a student is seen to be increasingly isolated, then this could be a cause for concern. This is especially true if the student used to be quite sociable and popular. As mental health and emotional wellbeing issues develop, it is common for students to withdraw from their friends and family, sometimes through a fear that someone will cotton on to their unhealthy behaviours of which they may feel ashamed or protective, and sometimes because they can no longer relate to the interests of their friends, which may seem trivial or unimportant by comparison to what is going on in the sufferer's own head.

Physical harm

Any form of physical injury could be an indicator of self-harm, including cuts, burns, bruises and scratches. These injuries should be of particular concern if they appear more than once, appear too neat to be accidental or do not seem to match the story that the child provides about how they were sustained. Such injuries may be the result of abuse being sustained by the child, or they may be the result of abuse the child is carrying out upon themselves.

Toilet trips

In many schools, the toilets are just about the only place of privacy, and so they are somewhere that some students will turn to when they need to escape because they simply are not managing. They can also be a safe place to privately self-harm, binge or purge. Students who always visit the toilet immediately following a meal may be purging themselves of their meal by vomiting or using laxatives.

Baggy or long clothing

Long, baggy or layered clothing can be used to hide extreme weight loss or weight gain or physical injuries sustained through self-harm. It is especially telling if a student chooses to continue to wear long sleeves in hot weather – it is possible they are hiding cuts or burns on their arms. Additionally, students who have suffered extreme weight loss tend to feel perpetually cold so may insist on wearing a large amount of clothing, even in hotter weather.

Another tell-tale sign can be constant wearing of a scarf which can be one of the few signs indicating that a student is suffering with bulimia. In cases where the student repeatedly induces vomiting, their face and neck can become swollen and puffy so they may choose to hide this by wearing a scarf.

Physical education/sport avoidance

Where a student is deeply ashamed of their body or wants to hide signs of weight loss, weight gain or self-harm, they will often take measures to avoid situations which involve changing in front of others. This will often result in them avoiding physical education and particularly swimming. Students also often have an additional incentive for avoiding physical education/sport which is that, regardless of the physical signs, sports staff and coaches can often be very astute at picking up mental health and emotional wellbeing problems, so a student who is not yet ready to talk about their concerns may avoid contact with sports staff.

Going out more or less

Some students will take to drinking excessively or taking drugs to try to obliterate their problems – this may result in them going out more than they used to and you may see signs of hangovers, or hear rumours of binge drinking. Conversely, a student who is suffering with an eating disorder may feel deeply uncomfortable about eating and drinking in front of other people which may lead to them avoiding a wide range of social situations. Students may also avoid going shopping with friends due to a reluctance to try on clothes in front of other people if they are ashamed of their body or trying to conceal weight change or self-harm.

Chewing gum or drinking water

Someone who is regularly vomiting may use chewing gum or water to mask the smell of vomit. Chewing gum or water may also be used in lieu of food, to occupy a student who is trying to restrict their food intake. Water is also often used by some sufferers to create a feeling of fullness despite not having eaten. However, it should be noted that, in more advanced cases of anorexia, it is not uncommon for sufferers to refuse to consume even water, for fear or weight gain or bloating.

Personality change
Students who exhibit an extreme personality change may be suffering with a mental health issue. You may observe that a student becomes very quiet, aggressive or negative. Personality change is commonly seen during adolescence, so it is common that these warning signs are written off as typical teenage behaviour. However, experienced school staff who have worked with a large number of students will have a good feel for what is a typical level of behaviour change and what is beyond what we might normally expect.

Poor hair, skin and nails
The poor nutrition that results from extreme dietary restriction, or regular purging, will often be reflected in a student's hair, skin and nails. Hair will look dull and lifeless and may begin to fall out in more extreme cases, skin is often sallow and nails are often brittle.

In more advanced cases of anorexia, you may also notice new growth of downy hair on a student's cheeks or a slight blue tinge to the extremities – especially noticeable in the fingernails – due to reduced circulation and a constant feeling of cold.

Toothache and headaches
Students who regularly make themselves sick may experience mouth ulcers or problems with their teeth due to enamel erosion resulting from the acidity of vomit. This can increase the likelihood of cavities and can leave the teeth very sensitive. Additionally, constant vomiting or laxative abuse often results in dehydration which may leave the student plagued by headaches.

Dizziness
Dizziness or fainting may be seen for a number of reasons depending on the underlying condition. Students who are restricting their food intake may simply become dizzy or faint due to lack of sustenance whilst those who are regularly vomiting or taking laxatives may be prone to dizziness resulting from dehydration. Additionally, fainting and dizzy spells may follow incidents of self-harm if the student experiences symptoms of shock (see box in Chapter 12).

Restricted eating and food rules

The most tell-tale sign of anorexia is restricted eating. Students with anorexia frequently impose strict and very low calorie limits on their food intake. It is also common for students with anorexia to impose a series of food rules on their diet which they will rigidly stick to. These will commonly include cutting out entire food groups; students with anorexia will often adopt a vegetarian or vegan lifestyle or a lactose-free or gluten-free lifestyle. These dietary choices are very socially acceptable ways of limiting food intake and often go unquestioned. Additionally, the student may gradually introduce more rules regarding what, when and how they can eat. These can become quite complex and ritualistic and the student may become very distressed if they are not allowed to adhere to these rules, which might include eating from a certain plate, chewing food a certain number of times or eating food only from the left-hand side of the plate, for example.

Scheduling activities during lunch

A really busy schedule during lunchtimes can leave a student without time to eat their lunch – or act as a distraction to stop them thinking about eating if they are forcing themselves to fast. It is easy for a busy student to fly under the radar if they are constantly tied up with extra-curricular activities. Some students might participate in a wide range of extracurricular activities, others might spend every lunchtime studying in the library or working out in the school gym.

Absence and lateness

Absenteeism and lateness are often very easy to track through school records. There can be a wide range of reasons why a student may be absent or late and self-harm or eating disorders are just one of a myriad of reasons. Specific reasons why self-harm and eating disorders might make a student late or absent include carrying out ritualistic self-harm or eating activities which take a long time and hold the student up, feeling the need to exercise at length after breakfast, finding it difficult to face school due to low self-esteem, weight shape and appearance concerns, or a general lack of motivation to get up and get to school, which could be the result of low mood or depression being suffered alongside self-harm or eating disorders.

LEARNING TO TAKE AWAY FROM THIS CHAPTER

- Earlier recognition of self-harming and eating-disordered behaviours improves the prognosis for treatment. An early pick-up will often result in a more rapid and more complete recovery.

- There are a range of physical and behavioural warning signs which indicate a student may be suffering from self-harm or eating disorders.

- It is important to be aware of the warning signs, but it is also important to follow our gut instincts. Even in the absence of specific warning signs, if we sense something is wrong, we should follow up with the student.

THINGS TO DO

- Consider whether there are any students currently in your care who are displaying physical or behavioural warning signs which indicate they may need support for self-harm or an eating disorder.

CHAPTER 7

Talking to Students Causing Concern

This chapter will enable you to:

- determine at what point you need to talk to a student causing concern
- paint a more complete picture of whether a student needs help
- confidently and sensitively start a conversation with a vulnerable student
- employ strategies for encouraging reluctant talkers to open up.

When should you say something?

Once you're aware of the risk factors and warning signs for eating disorders and self-harm you may find yourself noticing students at school who cause you some concern. You might be anxious that they could be in the early stages of an eating disorder or self-harming behaviour– but when should you say something? Should you sit back and monitor the situation until you're sure there's a problem or should you speak to them as soon as possible? It's a difficult question and, as much as anything, it will depend on your relationship with the student but there are some proactive steps you can take to get a better understanding of the most appropriate next steps.

Talk to other members of staff

My first port of call would often be to talk to other members of staff. If your school has clear policies and procedures in place which refer to self-harm or eating disorders then there will be a designated member of staff to whom mental health and emotional wellbeing concerns should be referred. If there is not a clearly designated member of staff in your school for these kinds of concerns then it is worth suggesting that this system is put in place.

> 'We've learned the hard way that we really need to talk to each other and have clear paths for referring concerns, no matter how minor – it's the only way to stop students falling through the gaps.'

It would be worth a conversation with the designated member of staff, where there is one, as it's possible that there is a known problem that is already being dealt with, and if not then they will be able to offer you clear guidance and support. It's also worth talking to other teachers who know the student well, to see if they've noticed anything amiss or if they are aware of any other reasons which might explain the warning signs you've noted.

> If you have regular meetings where you discuss students' academic performance and behaviour, why not add emotional wellbeing to the standard agenda? This way concerns about students can be aired at an early stage and you can quickly gauge whether others share your concern.

Try to get some information from their friends

Try to give the student's friends the opportunity to talk to you about any concerns they might have. Don't ask too many leading questions, but rather, provide them with an opportunity to tell you if there's something on their mind. You could try saying things like:

- I notice Amy's not been hanging around with you guys as much at break time, is everything okay?

- Amy's awfully quiet at the moment, is everything alright at home?

- Is there anything I can do to help Amy? She just doesn't seem herself at the moment, I wonder if I can help?

Often, if there is a problem, the student's friends will be aware that something is amiss and will have been worrying themselves, but not have known what to do. More often than not they will invite the opportunity to share their concerns with you and you're likely to get a much better insight into the problem this way.

> 'I'd been worried about Daniel for a while, but I didn't know who to tell or what to say. I wasn't sure exactly what I was worried about, it was just a sort of gut feeling you get when you know someone well. When my teacher

asked me if anything was wrong it was such a relief to finally tell someone and it was reassuring to know that he was going to keep an eye on Daniel and offer some help if it was needed.'

Don't wait too long

The key thing to remember with eating disorders and self-harm is that the more swiftly support is put in place, the better the long-term prognosis, as thought and behaviour patterns are far more difficult to overcome once they have had an opportunity to become fully entrenched. So if you're at all concerned about a student then a 'watching waiting' approach isn't really appropriate. After all, what are you waiting for – concrete proof that the student is making themselves sick, or are you watching until you've witnessed them cutting first hand? Far better that you go with your gut instinct and address the situation sooner rather than later. There is nothing to be lost this way. If your fears are misplaced, the student will be able to put your mind at rest and explain the reasons for the behaviours you've been noticing. And if you're right, then you're likely to find that in the early stages of their difficulties the student will be scared and confused and far more likely to invite some form of help or support.

> 'I got it very wrong. I was aware there was an issue but I thought it might pass. I was keeping an eye on the student to see if things got better or worse. Things got worse. I finally ended up having the conversation in accident and emergency after a serious self-harm incident.'

Create opportunities for them to speak to you

Rather than hauling the student to one side or insisting that they stay behind after class for an unspecified meeting with you, try to create more natural opportunities for the student to talk to you privately. This will mean they are more relaxed, and if you're able to engineer a situation where they feel they've instigated the conversation they will feel more in control and be more likely to open up. This doesn't need to be anything too clever; simply asking them to stay behind for five minutes to discuss last night's homework is enough – then you should actually discuss the homework before asking casually 'Are you okay? You seem awfully quiet' or something similar, which will hopefully lead to them talking to you but, if not, make sure you extend an open invitation for them to talk to you if they need help: 'Well, I'm glad you're okay, but if ever you do need someone to talk to then remember you can always find me in my room on Tuesday at lunchtime.' This will give the student the chance to go away and think about whether they're ready to share their problems and gives them a concrete time and place to return to when they're ready. Just make sure you are where you say you'll be. Even at the point at which they are ready to accept help, students often find it very difficult to make the first move so it is perfectly appropriate to ask the student periodically if they are okay and whether you can support them. They may refuse the offer of help the first, second and twenty-third time…but they will often accept your support eventually.

'When he first asked if he could help me I wasn't ready. The next time I wanted to talk but didn't believe he could possibly care about someone as worthless as me. But he kept asking and eventually I guess I realized that, if he didn't care, he wouldn't ask, so I took the plunge and started talking.'

Don't be confrontational

Whatever you do, don't just barrel up to the student in question and say, 'I'm worried you might have an eating disorder.' All this will do is alienate you from the student and remove any possibility that they might have been willing to confide in you. In fact I'd advocate not using the words 'eating disorder' or 'self-harm' at all during your early discussions.

'I try not to set my expectations too high for those first discussions. You can't expect a student to talk about their most difficult issues before they've built up their trust in you. I never tell them my suspicions that they've been self-harming but instead aim to create a supportive environment where they feel safe talking to me. When you're trying to help someone overcome self-harm, you're entering into a long-term relationship so it makes no sense to rush the early stages. Instead, look to build solid foundations.'

Try to create an environment where you do most of the listening and focus on allowing the student to talk. You might not get to the nub of the problem during your first conversation, but at this point, trust is the most important thing. Invite them to come and talk to you again tomorrow or next week. Soon you'll find that if the student trusts you they will allow you enough insight to plan what you need to do next. The relationship you work hard to build during these early stages will form a firm basis for weeks or months of recovery.

Positive communication

If a student chooses to talk to you, or responds to your offers of support about their eating or harming behaviours, it's a real sign of trust and it demonstrates that they're ready to be listened to. The most important thing you can do is provide them with the opportunity to talk. No one expects you to know all the answers, but simply by actively listening you're doing a really important job.

Whilst it can seem quite daunting, especially if you're not used to handling these types of disclosures, here are some simple guidelines you can follow to ensure that the student feels supported and listened to:

Make sure there's no time pressure

A student will have to build up quite a lot of courage to have a conversation with you about their eating or harming thoughts and behaviours, so if you suddenly have to run off to do lunch duty after five minutes it can really shake their confidence. Although you may legitimately need to be somewhere else, their low self-esteem is likely to make the student interpret the situation negatively and assume that you aren't interested in what they have to say or that you don't want to help them and that they don't deserve to be helped.

To avoid this, make sure you have plenty of interruption-free time before you sit down to talk to a student. This can feel frustrating if a student says they want to talk to you but due to your other commitments you have to send them away until later – but if you make it crystal clear that it's because you want to have enough time to really listen to what they have to say, and offer what support you can, then they will understand. You must agree a time and place to meet again as soon as possible and ensure that you are where you say you'll be.

If for any reason you can't keep to the agreed time or place, you must let the student know – but don't give them a hard time if they don't stick to the meeting time, just offer to reschedule when you next see them.

Remove all distractions

You need to focus 100 per cent on the student for the next few minutes. You need to really listen to them, which means removing any distractions. Turn your phone off, turn your computer screen off. Make sure your door is shut and put up a note asking people not to disturb you (if your position/school policy allows).

> 'I always make a point of saying "I'm just going to turn my phone off. It's really important that I can focus fully on this conversation."'

Actively demonstrating to the student that you are making them a priority sends a very clear message at a time when they are likely to be in great need of reassurance and may be confused about what is going on. It might feel funny, but just giving a commentary of the steps you are taking so you can focus on them will help them to realize that you're taking them seriously.

Think about seating arrangements

Try to ensure that the seating arrangement lends itself to an open conversation. Sitting either side of a desk can feel overly formal and intimidating – a round table or no table at all lends itself far better to sharing thoughts and feelings. Consider sitting at right angles to or next to the student instead of directly across from them as this can make it easier for the student to open up – in day-to-day life we often have our most intimate conversations whilst sitting next to someone in a car, or sitting side by side rather than sat across at a table. It's because we feel more comfortable and you can mimic this with your student.

> 'I have a little nook in my office with comfortable chairs and a round low table which I always ensure has tissues and water to hand. Students often comment on how welcoming it feels.'

If your role means that you regularly have sensitive conversations and it's possible to set up an informal seating area then you're likely to find this makes a real difference. However, by thinking carefully, you can adapt almost any room, with any furniture, to suit your needs.

Use appropriate body language

Keep your body language open and approachable during the conversation. You need to make it clear that you're paying attention and that you're not horrified by what you're hearing. Don't cross your arms and legs as this can come across as cold and defensive. When we feel comfortable with someone we tend to mirror their body language; if it feels appropriate to do so, making a conscious effort to do this can help both you and the student to relax.

A key thing to consider is eye contact. You may need to consciously focus on maintaining a natural level of eye contact. Too much eye contact and the student may feel you're staring at them:

> 'He wouldn't stop staring. It made me feel so uncomfortable.'

Too little and they may think you're repulsed by them:

> 'She was so disgusted by what I told her that she couldn't bear to look at me.'

Make a conscious effort to make occasional eye contact if it feels appropriate, and try not to instantly look away if a student shows you injuries or scars as this may be interpreted very negatively.

Prove that you're listening

You can show that you're listening quite naturally by nodding your head, making 'listening noises' like 'uhuh' or 'mmm' periodically. Every now and then you should paraphrase what the student has said to you to show that you've been paying attention and understand.

> 'I don't like to take notes, as I worry that this is intimidating, so it's important for me to keep summarizing what is being said. I summarize every few minutes and take real care to untangle anything I've misunderstood – this happens surprisingly often; never make assumptions about what a student means.'

Never be afraid to explore your misunderstandings with the student, or to ask them to clarify or explore something further. If they've not explained it well the first time it can often be due to the fact that they've not voiced it before and may only just be beginning to understand their own thoughts and feelings themselves. Repeating, clarifying and rephrasing will not only aid your understanding, it will aid the student's.

Keep your talking to a minimum

The student should be talking at least three-quarters of the time. If that's not the case then you need to redress the balance. You are here to listen, not to talk. Sometimes the conversation may lapse into silence. Try not to give in to the urge to fill the gap, but rather wait until the student does so.

> 'Sometimes it's hard to explain what's going on in my head – it doesn't make a lot of sense and I've kind of gotten used to keeping myself to myself. But just 'cos I'm struggling to find the right words doesn't mean you should help me. Just keep quiet, I'll get there in the end.'

Taking time to listen will often lead to students exploring their feelings more deeply. Of course, you should interject occasionally, perhaps with questions to the student to explore certain topics they've touched on more deeply, or to show that you understand and are supportive. Don't feel an urge to over-analyse the situation or try to offer answers. This all comes later. For now your role is simply one of supportive listener. So make sure you're listening.

'She listened, and I mean REALLY listened. She didn't interrupt me or ask me to explain myself or anything, she just let me talk and talk and talk. I had been unsure about talking to anyone but I knew quite quickly that I'd chosen the right person to talk to and that it would be a turning point.'

Ideas for encouraging reluctant talkers to open up

Some students will be very reluctant to talk, or may feel incredibly uncomfortable talking about their thoughts and feelings. Based on approaches that have worked for others or which have been advocated by students, I've outlined some general guidelines below:

Have realistic expectations

It's important to keep your expectations in check. Many people feel disappointed if a student won't instantly open up to them during an initial conversation but, unless the student has come to you, it's relatively unlikely that they're ready to discuss their difficulties. Even if they've instigated the conversation, they may not know what to say or how to say it or may be held back by uncertainty as to how you'll respond.

Not eliciting a disclosure from a student during a first conversation is not a failure. You need to build a relationship where the student feels that they can trust you enough to talk openly. Taking time to build a solid relationship will stand you in good stead for the months ahead, so this is not time wasted, and simply knowing that someone cares enough to talk to them, even if they've not told you what's wrong yet, will be deeply reassuring for many students.

'It wasn't until the fourth time we sat down and talked that I owned up about my self-harm. I'm pretty sure she knew by that point but it was hard to find the words to tell her, it took me a while just to feel comfortable talking to her at all. When I finally told her I felt so much relief. I think if I'd said something before I was ready I'd have panicked and gone home and cut.'

If a student does disclose right away then that's great but, if not, then agree a time to meet again and just keep talking to them until they've built up enough trust to confide in you. Once you are confident that the student feels safe talking to you, you can begin to guide the conversation in the direction of your concerns if you feel the student will not find their way there otherwise, but don't rush this step.

Reassure

Take time to reassure the student. Make sure they realize that you are genuinely interested in hearing what they have to say and that you have made time to listen to them. Students worry a lot that when they share their concerns we'll over-react, dismiss their worries or judge them. Reassure them that none of these things will happen.

> 'I didn't tell anyone for ages because I thought they'd think I was a nutter and they'd never look at me the same way again.'

Depending on the student it can be helpful to tell them that you've supported students in similar situations before – for some students this is reassuring as they can feel very alone and like there is no way out. Knowing that other people have been through similar difficulties and pulled through can make them feel better. Other students consider their problems to be completely unique and are offended or affronted by the idea that anyone else could understand or that you think that their problems or responses are typical, so take the lead from your knowledge of your student, and the signs they are giving as to whether you choose to allude to similar situations with other students in the past.

Talk about what will happen next

It can be very helpful to be open and honest with a student from the start about what the likely next steps are if they do disclose a problem to you. Students are often very concerned about what will happen and are unclear about what school policy dictates, or have made wildly inaccurate assumptions:

> 'I was certain that if I told my form tutor he would have to send a memo to every member of staff. Once he explained that that would NOT happen, I felt more ready to start talking…'

Talking a student through what will happen with regard to confidentiality is particularly important as this is often a key concern. You can also talk to them about how you will be able to follow up in terms of support, for example, if you'll be able to refer them to the school counsellor. Once the student is armed with information about what will happen if they do make a disclosure, they can make a more informed decision about whether they're ready to do so. Students may choose not to disclose this time but to go away and come back once they've considered what you've told them. In the meantime it can be helpful to provide them with sources of support they can access, such as 24-hour helplines or websites with online counsellors – students will often choose to disclose first to an anonymous source. This can be a helpful way of them practising what they need to say in a safe environment.

Start with small talk

Don't feel like you should launch straight into attempting to talk about the key concerns you have about the student. In fact, it would be inappropriate to do so as the student would not have a chance to relax and build their trust in you. Many people find that idle small talk about what was on TV last night or a popular film, for example, can be a great way to get a student talking in general, and that once they've started talking, and you've started listening, the conversation will often move relatively naturally to the topic that you both realize is the reason you're here.

Sometimes you can draw inspiration directly from TV or film to help you start to understand how the student is feeling. Talking about the feelings and actions of different characters on TV and in films and books can often offer a real glimpse into how the student is feeling and a natural segue into talking about the issues which are of real concern.

Use silence

Silence is a fantastic tool and one we shouldn't be afraid of. It can feel very, very uncomfortable. When we're the one doing the listening, silence is excruciating and even short silences can feel like a very long time. But try to resist the urge to fill them. Whilst all you can hear is silence, for the student, they probably hear anything but silence. They have a million thoughts running through their head: What should they tell you? How should they say it? What will you say? They will be buzzing with questions. It can take quite some time for them to formulate their thoughts and to put into words what they want to say. If you resist the urge to talk then you'll find that, in most instances, the student will usually start talking eventually, having thought very carefully about what they should say next.

Ask open questions

Open questions are a great way to encourage a student to explore their thoughts and feelings. You can start with open questions about more general topics just to get the student talking and later on move on to open questions which help you to understand the underlying problems. The great thing about open questions is that they require a more extensive answer than 'yes' or 'no' or 'twenty-three', so they can be great for facilitating exploration by the student. Open questions which might be appropriate include:

- You've not been yourself lately, how can I help?

- How can I support you?

- What do you think we should do next?

- Why do you think that might be?

- Please can you explain a bit more about that?

- Is there a reason you feel that way?

Constantly using open questions can begin to feel a little emotionally exhausting for the student though; if you sense this is happening then revert to closed questions, or make use of silence briefly. You should also take care not to ask leading questions.

Explore things through the third person

It is often far easier for a student to explore their concerns through the third person. Having to openly talk about their thoughts and behaviours using 'I' can be very daunting, but you can often begin to gain an understanding by posing questions which explore how a friend or parent might be feeling about the student's behaviour lately, or about how the student might feel about this behaviour if they noted it in a friend. For example:

- Your friends are worried – do you know why?

- What do you think your friends would say if they knew you felt this way?

- How do you think your parents feel about that?

- Do you think your parents are worried about how much you're eating? Why?

- Have your friends commented on your injuries? What have they said?

- What would you advise your friend if they were burning themselves?

- How would it make you feel if you knew your friend felt as low as you've been feeling?

- How do you think you could help a friend who was self-harming?

This can sometimes lead to quite defensive answers, but at least it gets the student talking. For example, asking a student why they think their friends are worried about them might receive an angry comeback along the lines of 'They're probably saying that I'm not eating enough, but it's complete rubbish. They should keep their noses out.' A defensive response like this can feel negative but it gives you a lot to explore with the student...you could go on to ask 'What makes them think you've not been eating enough?' and continue to ask open questions to gain an understanding of when or where the student is eating. Equally you could explore their anger at their friends' concern: 'Do you think it's inappropriate for your friends to be concerned about you?' or 'Do your friends often worry about you? Why?'

Do an activity

Another approach to get students talking is to move to a situation where talking is not the central activity. Having a conversation with an adult about a really difficult topic can feel very full-on, so having something to take your mind off it can facilitate discussion. It's useful to know a bit about the student because if you happen to know that they enjoy a particular subject which lends itself to emotional expression then that can be hugely helpful – if a student likes to draw, paint or sculpt, for example, then talking to them whilst they are doing these activities can mean that they feel more relaxed and that the conversation is less confrontational. Equally, some people find that simply going for a walk, or playing a simple board game or similar can make the situation feel less intense and facilitate talking.

Remind them why they're here

A simple technique which can often work wonders and get students really thinking is to simply remind them that they are sitting in your office out of their own free will: that they chose to come, they chose to sit and, so far, they have not chosen to leave. This can be especially effective if they are actively protesting about the idea of talking to you. Of course, you have to be fully prepared that the student may then choose to get up and walk away. If they do so then they will often return at a later date ready to talk. Often it has not occurred to them that they have a choice in all of this. That can feel daunting at first but it can often help them to realize that things do not have to continue the way they are. This can lead to them returning to talk to you another day. If this doesn't happen, it doesn't mean they haven't thought of doing so but they may be too anxious to make the first move, so it can make a lot of sense to offer them an appointment time and accept that they may or may not turn up.

You might not be the best person for the job

Finally, sometimes a student doesn't talk to us because we are not the most appropriate person for the job. This is no reflection on us, but students will each have their own preferences about who they would feel most comfortable talking to and this is not always in line with staffing structures at school. Ideally any member of staff should be ready and able to talk to a student in need.

If you feel that a student you are concerned about may be more likely to open up to someone else then you can still play a role by talking to the student in an attempt to identify someone they'd like to talk to and approaching that member of staff to see if they'd be happy to talk to the student. You can then offer support to the member of staff involved so that they feel confident enough to have the conversation and follow up appropriately. Students will often feel especially comfortable talking to members of staff with whom they have an especially positive relationship. This might be the teacher of a subject they excel in, or perhaps a sports coach. Don't make any assumptions, have an open discussion with the student and help them to identify someone appropriate and don't feel that this means you've failed because, in fact, you are enabling them to open up to someone which may not have happened if you had not become involved.

LEARNING TO TAKE AWAY FROM THIS CHAPTER

- If you have concerns about a student, it is in the student's best interests that you, or another member of staff, offer them some support as soon as possible.

- Colleagues and peers of the student can offer helpful insight if you're not sure if your concerns are valid.

- Your role is to listen to the student's concerns – there are several strategies you can use to show a student that they are your priority, that you're taking the conversation seriously and that you're actively listening to them.

- It's important to have realistic expectations – a student may not instantly open up about their problems and we may not be the best person for them to speak to.

THINGS TO DO

- If there are any students you are currently concerned about, decide how and when you will move things forwards so they can access the support they need.

- Think about how you can make your office or classroom feel like an inviting and undaunting place for a student to talk about their difficulties.

- Practise active listening – developing this skill with friends and colleagues will mean you are in a better position when you next have a sensitive conversation with a student.

CHAPTER 8

Responding to Disclosures and Self-Harm Incidents

This chapter will enable you to:

- support a student appropriately if they confide in you about self-harm or eating disorder concerns

- respond appropriately if a student shows you injuries caused by self-harm

- retain a student's trust without promising you'll keep their concerns confidential

- overcome student objections to informing their parents about their difficulties

- take appropriate next steps following a student disclosure.

How you can support

When a student opens up to you about a mental health or emotional wellbeing difficulty, there are a few things you should bear in mind throughout your initial conversation as well as any subsequent conversations which can help the student to feel supported.

Make time

Making time to talk to a student sends a powerful message – it says that you care about them and that you take their situation seriously.

'I was surprised that he would make time just for me. I didn't think anyone would care enough to do that. It was a turning point…the first time I began to wonder if maybe I was worth caring about.'

We live in a very busy time and it's uncommon for most students to have the undivided attention of the trusted adults in their life for any significant period of time, so making the effort to make the student your sole focus for a set period of time will reap dividends in terms of relationship and trust-building.

Listen

Above all else, you need to listen. The student may never have spoken to anyone about their difficulties before, so confiding in you is a very big step. More than anything they need a chance to talk, to explore why they're going through the difficult thoughts and behaviours they're experiencing.

Don't judge

Students will often hold back from confiding in anyone about self-harm or eating-disordered behaviours because they fear inappropriate responses or judgement. They worry that their concerns will be dismissed as insignificant or attention seeking or that people will over-react, perhaps assuming that they are suicidal. They also worry because of the negative stigma that mental health issues inappropriately carry and think that their disclosure will change how people think about them.

> 'I wanted to talk to my English teacher because I like him and trust him more than anyone else at school. But then I thought "but I like him, and he likes me. Won't he think I'm like some kind of freak if I tell him this? He'll think I'm a nutter or a loony and he'll never want to go near me again."'

This is part of a wider problem and tackling the stigma associated with mental health issues could usefully form part of your wider curriculum, but, in terms of the individual student, it's important to reassure them that what they've disclosed does not impact on how you think about them as an individual. It doesn't mean you'll treat them differently or like them less. You'll do your best to support them but you'll never judge them.

Persevere

It's important to continue to offer support, even if your offers are met with anger of indifference. You shouldn't always take a student's response at face value:

> 'The anorexic voice in my head was telling me to push help away, so I was saying no. But there was a tiny part of me that wanted to get better. I just couldn't say it out loud or else I'd have to punish myself.'

Despite the fact that a student has confided in you, and may even have expressed a desire to get on top of their difficulties, this doesn't mean they'll readily accept help. Their difficulties may ensure they resist any form of help for as long as they possibly can. Don't be offended or upset if your offers of help are met with anger, indifference or insolence: it's the illness talking, not the student.

> 'I feel so ashamed when I look back. She was so lovely and I was so, so… horrible. I even spat at her one time. All she wanted to do was help but I wasn't ready. But she kept trying and eventually I was ready, I guess she kind of wore me down. I'll always be grateful that she stuck by me. I couldn't have got better on my own.'

However negatively your offers of support are responded to, they usually have a real impact on the student's self-esteem and readiness to change, enabling them to slowly understand that they are worth helping, and it is possible and desirable for things to change.

Be honest
It's important that you're able to build up a trusting relationship with the student where they feel that when they are with you, they are in a safe and supportive relationship where they can begin to explore their issues and ways to overcome them. In order to protect this relationship it's vital that you are completely honest with students. If they feel you are not being honest with them then they will be far less inclined to be honest with you.

Specific topics you may need to take care to be honest about include:

CONFIDENTIALITY
Students know that you can't always keep their confidence, but unless you are honest about this upfront they can feel like you've been dishonest with them. Suddenly saying after a 30-minute conversation 'Of course we'll need to tell your parents' is the type of thing that could cause your relationship to break down completely.

> 'It's fine. I know you're probably going to tell my mum, but don't lie about it. Tell me before I start talking then I can decide how much I actually want to say to you.'

Ideas about effectively managing the issue of confidentiality are shared later in this chapter. If a student does not feel ready to share their concerns with you once they learn that you cannot keep their confidentiality then they may find an anonymous helpline or online forum is a good alternative. A student who shares their concerns in an anonymous environment will often gradually develop the confidence needed to speak to someone face to face.

'I started the conversation by explaining the limits of confidentiality. She wasn't sure if what she was going to tell me would be something I'd have to tell her parents so I suggested she called Childline to discuss it. The next morning she came to find me again and this time she was ready to talk. She said she knew I'd have to tell other people, but the counsellor from Childline had explained the positive sides to this and she felt more ready now.'

HOW RAPIDLY YOU CAN HELP

Some students will come to you expecting you to wave a magic wand and make everything better. They need to know that you will do your best to support them but it will not happen instantly and it will take a lot of hard work and determination on their part.

HOW DIFFICULT YOU FIND THE SITUATION

If you've known a student for a period of months or years, it can be deeply upsetting and unsettling to hear them talking about ways in which they are struggling, especially where behaviours like self-harm are involved. It's okay, and often helpful, to be honest with a student and let them know that it makes you sad that they feel the need to cope with their emotions in this way. If you're not straightforward about the impact their disclosure has had on you then your response may be misinterpreted. Explaining that you find the behaviour upsetting because you care about the student and that you actively want to support them to find alternatives can be affirming for a student to hear, though care needs to be taken to ensure the student doesn't end up feeling guilty.

Students appreciate an upfront approach and it makes them feel that you are treating them like an adult rather than a child, which tends to go down well.

Try to understand

The concept of eating-disordered or self-harming behaviour can seem completely alien if you've never experienced these difficulties first hand. You may find yourself wondering why on earth someone would do these things to themselves, but don't explore those feelings with the student. Acknowledging the seriousness of the situation but reacting calmly will show the student that it is not too horrible to bear. Listen calmly to what they're saying and encourage them to talk and you'll slowly start to understand what steps they might be ready to take in order to start making some changes.

Remember the real child

People often feel that once they've been diagnosed with a mental health or emotional wellbeing difficulty, it's like walking around with a massive label attached to them which obscures their former personality. Many people see them only as 'The Bulimic' or 'The Self-Harmer' and forget about all the things that make the student unique.

It's important that we take steps to remember the 'real child', the child who we knew before these difficulties. This will help us during recovery as it will enable us to draw on aspects of the student's skills and interests which may help them engage in the recovery process. It will also help them to remember who they were to start with and, therefore, who they're aiming to be again when they're fully recovered. It's common for students to experience a large degree of physical and emotional withdrawal from people and activities they used to enjoy engaging in, but never lose sight of these. Use them to engage and motivate the student and encourage others to do the same.

Take a child-centred approach

For students with mental health and emotional wellbeing issues, it can often feel like everything is happening to them rather than with them. This can make them feel out of control of their own life and exacerbate their difficulties. Recovery is far more likely to be successful and sustainable if the student is fully involved during every step of the process.

> 'I was worried how she'd react, but she just listened then said, "How can I support you?" No one had asked me that before and it made me realize that she cared. Between us we thought of some really practical things she could do to help me stop self-harming.'

Involve the students in meetings; talk to them about next steps; discuss with them who should be told what; ask them what support they need. Do all that you can to ensure that the student is at the heart of their own recovery, not on the periphery.

Be practical

Where possible, take a practical approach. Listen to what the student tells you in terms of their current difficulties and needs and try to work with them to come up with practical approaches to address these needs. It's often helpful to write simple action plans to help keep things focused. This can give you a sense of control and make the student feel safer and as though something is happening to move things forwards.

Be prepared for setbacks

Recovery tends not to be a linear process; be prepared for this and be honest with the student that this is likely to be the reality. Every time the student has a setback, this is an opportunity for them to learn about their triggers and the best responses to strengthen the next leg of their recovery.

How to respond if a student shows you their injuries

Many people feel very uncomfortable about the idea of talking to a student about their self-harm and feel even more uncomfortable about the idea of being shown injuries. It can be shocking to be confronted with injuries or scars, especially if the student is someone you have known for some time and have come to care about. Your feelings may range from upset to angry to confused but, no matter how you feel, it's important that the student feels supported. I am often asked what you should say and do and what you should avoid saying if a student shows you their injuries or scars. The truth is that there is no definitive right or wrong answer to this and it really depends on your relationship with the student and what your gut tells you is appropriate, but here are some suggestions:

Acknowledge how hard this must have been

Showing someone their injuries will be a very significant step for the student and a terrifying one, as they will fear judgement and ridicule. Acknowledging that this will have been a difficult step and thanking them for trusting you enough to show you will give the student a clear message that you are on their side, that you value them and that you understand a little bit about the difficulties they're facing.

Don't ask them what happened

At some point in your relationship with the student, you might both be ready to discuss the intricacies of their self-harming rituals but the first time they show you their injuries is unlikely to be that moment. At this point asking what happened is not going to tell you anything and may alienate the student, who will probably think it's pretty obvious what happened.

'I showed him the cuts on my leg and he was like "What happened?" and I was like "Seriously? What do you think happened? Have you not been listening for the last 40 minutes or what?"'

Don't expect them to understand why they did it

Some students, especially those who are more advanced in their recoveries, may be able to explain their motivations for self-harming very eloquently. But most, especially in the early days, find it hard to understand what's going on themselves, let alone explain it to someone else. 'Why did you do it?' is not a very helpful question as it can leave the student confused and upset and can also suggest disapproval on your part.

Don't comment on the seriousness of their injuries

You should never pass comment on the severity or lack thereof of a student's injuries. It's not relevant unless there is an urgent need for first aid or a hospital admission. A student who cuts deeply is not necessarily any more or less distressed than a student who shows you minor-looking scratches. If the student thinks that you are passing judgement on how severely they've harmed themselves – either that their injuries are disproportionately severe compared to the cause of their distress, or that their injuries are so minor that they 'may not constitute self-harm' – then you are likely to alienate and upset them.

'She'd listened really intently and I thought she was going to help me right up until I showed her where I'd been cutting. I swear she almost laughed. She passed some comment about how she was relieved that I hadn't cut any deeper but I could tell she thought I was just mucking about. I cut much more deeply the next time to make sure she knew I was serious.'

Rather than passing any judgement about injuries, just treat them as fact – these injuries are symptomatic of the student's underlying issues and your key concern (once any first aid implications are dealt with) is to help the student to find different ways of coping rather than over-analysing the specific self-harming approach they are currently taking.

Don't over-react or trivialize it

Students often fear that they'll be seen as either attention seeking or suicidal if they disclose their injuries. Try to ensure that your response indicates neither of these things, but rather that you want to support the student.

Don't tell them to stop

We would never expect a student to instantly overcome an addiction to drugs, yet many people think it's appropriate to expect them to stop self-harming instantly. For many students, self-harm is the one thing that helps them to manage to make it through each day and prevents them from taking more drastic action. Asking them to stop will either set them up for failure or could potentially fuel more dangerous behaviours.

> 'I expected him to ask me to stop, but he made a point of explaining that he thought that was an unrealistic expectation, but that he hoped we could work together to start to find different ways for me to manage my feelings. That felt achievable.'

Don't make superficial comments

Upon seeing someone's injuries for the first time, many people think it will prove helpful to make superficial comments such as 'But how will you look in your wedding dress?' or 'You'll never be able to wear a bikini on holiday if you carry on like this!' in order to motivate them to stop. These superficialities will not compete with the underlying distress which is causing the student to self-harm; they will, however, give them yet another thing to worry and feel guilty about.

> 'I was like what the f***! I've told you I've been self-harming because I hate myself so deeply and you're talking about wedding dresses. Listen to yourself. No one is going to want to marry this piece of s*** anyway.'

First aid

If a student lets you see their injuries then it is worth noting whether they've been looked after appropriately. It may be appropriate at some point in the conversation to share with them some ideas about wound care. If the wounds are in clear need of medical attention, this must be a first priority.

Maintaining the student's trust without promising confidentiality

The issue of confidentiality is a key concern for many school staff. Of course, we all know that if there is any possibility of a student doing themselves harm then we simply cannot keep their confidentiality – it could put both the student and your job in jeopardy. However, you can be sure that if a student does build up the courage to talk to you about their eating disorder or self-harming, then one of their first pleas will be 'Please don't tell anyone.'

It can feel frustrating not being able to agree to this caveat and it always feels entirely possible that you will lose the student's hard-earned trust if you refuse, but being upfront and honest now will pay dividends in the long run. If you promised to keep their trust then break that promise, the fall-out would be far greater than if you were honest from the start.

Involve the student

In order to retain the student's trust you need to involve them in the process of informing others – always consider who, what, why and how with the student before you disclose details of their difficulties to anyone else.

WHO SHOULD YOU TALK TO?

Discuss with the student who you think needs to be told about their difficulties. This list will depend on your school's policies and procedures and how severe the student's eating disorder or self-harm is, but people who you might want to consider informing are:

- the student's parents

- the person with lead responsibility for mental health in your school

- the student's form tutor

- the school nurse/counsellor

- a close friend of the student.

The student may have people to add to this list, or advice to offer about which of their parents it is best to talk to, if they perceive one as more likely to be supportive than the other, for example.

WHY SHOULD YOU TALK TO THEM?

Talk to the student about why or why not specific people should be told about their difficulties. You are likely to come up against a lot of opposition when you suggest telling their parents as students are often concerned about worrying their parents or think they will be upset or angry. Eating disorders and self-harm are both very secretive difficulties. It will have taken a huge amount of courage for the student to have confided in you, so the thought of telling other people is likely to terrify them. You need to be able to give justifications for sharing the information with each new person. These may include:

- you have to, it's school policy that X should be told

- they will be able to offer support

- they may have been worrying about the student and will be relieved that steps are being taken to address things

- they need to know so they can make certain allowances for the student.

WHAT WILL YOU SAY?

As well as agreeing who you should speak to and why, you should discuss with the student exactly what information will be shared. It's likely that the student has told you a lot more than needs to be passed on and there may be some aspects of what they've shared that they consider to be embarrassing or highly personal and would prefer you left out when passing the information on. Between you and the student you should be able to agree what each person needs to know in order to be able to offer the most appropriate support or follow up. In general the student will feel happiest if you share a minimum of information. As they become more comfortable with talking about their difficulties they may be happier to share more information.

HOW WILL YOU TELL THEM?

Talk to the student about how the people you've agreed to tell will be told about their difficulties. Do they want you to pass on the information? Would they like to do it themselves? Would they like you to support them in having the conversation? Perhaps they'd like to work with you to write a letter if they think a face-to-face conversation would simply be too difficult. Think too about where the conversation should take place: at school? At home? Outside school? All these seemingly small factors can make a huge difference to a student who is panicking about their secret 'getting out'.

If the student wants to tell their parents themselves, it's important that you give them a timeframe in which to do so and that you follow up with the student and their parents after that time has passed. A student should not be made to feel they've failed if they do not manage to talk to their parents, but you should look again at how this approach can best be made. Often students confide in a member of school staff specifically so that they don't have to tell their parents about their difficulties themselves, so always ensure you offer to have the first conversation on behalf of, or alongside, the student, in case this is what they would find most comfortable.

Allow the student to feel in control

The important thing about this process is that you're enabling the student to feel like they're retaining some control of the process. Of course you'll have to do some steering to make sure that the appropriate people are informed, but if you work with the student and allow them to input into the process then they will feel like you're on their side and that this process is happening with them, not to them, which is a very important distinction for someone who is coming to terms with eating-disordered or self-harming thoughts and behaviours – and whose symptoms are likely to be exacerbated any time they feel out of control.

When not to tell

If a student leads you to believe through either their words or their actions that they may be suffering abuse or neglect at home, then it would be inappropriate to inform parents about your concerns about the student as this may exacerbate their difficulties. Instead, you should work alongside your school's child protection lead to follow up the situation as appropriate.

WORKING WITH STUDENTS POST 16

Another possible exception is older students, and in particular those over 16. You need to be guided by your school or college's policy which may say that parents of students of all ages need to be informed about issues like self-harm and eating disorders, but often this is more ambiguous when it comes to working with older students. At this point, I find the most useful acid test of the best course of action is 'Would my actions stand up in court?' If you are absolutely confident that you could defend your decision not to inform parents in court, then you may choose to pursue this course of action. However, I would always inform another member of staff and look for a second opinion. In order to protect ourselves, it usually makes sense to escalate concerns within the school staffing structure and to follow the guidance of more experienced colleagues. Unless there is suspicion of neglect or abuse, I would always advocate informing parents and working with them during the student's recovery. Perhaps surprisingly, I consider this to be more, rather than less, important when working with students who are older because they are closer to the school leaving age. If their parents are unaware of their difficulties, when they no longer have the support and stability provided by the school environment and staff, then it is likely that their mental health and emotional wellbeing issues will escalate as they undergo the challenging transition to employment or university.

Overcoming objections to informing parents

A good relationship with parents can make a huge difference when you're supporting a student with eating-disordered or self-harming thoughts and behaviours. The student, their parents and the school should all be working together towards the common goal of helping the student to recover. However, students are often reluctant for their parents to be informed and involved for a variety of reasons. Here are some suggestions for overcoming common objections you're likely to face:

They won't understand

This is a common concern for students who may be at an age where they feel at quite a distance from their parents. They may feel that their parents won't understand the problem and will be in no position to help or support so there is no point in telling them. In this instance you need to explain to the student that their parents probably won't understand right away – but it's unlikely that anyone could – do they think that even their best friend can *really* understand? Explain that their parents will want to learn to understand and to offer their support. Make it clear that you'll be there to support the student whilst they explain things to their parents.

'I knew my parents wouldn't get it, and I didn't have the words to explain it to them…but my teacher told them with me. She answered all their questions and they did begin to understand after a little while.'

I don't want to worry them

Students often believe that by keeping their eating disorder or self-harming a secret from their parents, this will prevent them worrying about it. You should gently explain to the student that it is likely that their parents are already worried about them – perhaps mention tell-tale signs that had got you worried which their parents will probably have noticed too. Then explain that by telling their parents about their eating disorder or self-harm it will help them to worry less because you'll all be working together to do something positive about it.

'When I told my mum she just looked at me and said, "I already knew, but I didn't know what to say or do." She'd been worried for a while.'

They'll be angry

Parents are quite likely to get either angry or upset when they learn about their child's eating disorder or self-harm. This is a fairly normal reaction to being told such emotional news about someone you love. Explaining to the student that this phase is almost always very short-lived, and is usually rapidly followed by a concerned but supportive attitude, will help them to realize that telling their parents is not such a bad idea. Reiterate that you are happy to support the student and help them talk to their parents, and discuss how you can make the meeting as calm as possible. Lots of tea and tissues and an informal set-up usually help.

> 'As a parent myself I can totally understand the angry responses we get from parents sometimes. I think it's really more a sign of frustration, fear or guilt that they should have noticed or somehow stopped it happening. The usual cycle seems to be anger, then upset, then a desperate desire to listen, ask questions and do whatever they can to help. Parents often need as much TLC as the kids at this point.'

Thinking about the best way to inform parents can make a huge difference. Thinking about who tells them, what they need to know and the benefits of telling them can make a huge difference to the student's attitude. The one thing you must not do is promise not to tell parents and then go back on your promise as that is a sure-fire way to destroy your delicate relationship with the student.

What next?

Once your discussion with the student is coming to an end, there are a few useful things that you can do to wrap up:

Acknowledge how hard this was

Thank the student for trusting you enough to share their concerns with you and acknowledge how hard the conversation must have been for them. This may have been the first time they've spoken about their self-harm or eating disorder thoughts and feelings and it will have been far from easy. Acknowledging that will help them to realize that you understand a little bit about the enormity of this disclosure for them.

> 'Talking about my bingeing for the first time was the hardest thing I ever did. When I was done talking, my teacher looked me in the eye and said, "That must have been really tough" – he was right, it was, but it meant so much that he realized what a big deal it was for me.'

Summarize what the student has said

Summarizing what the student has said will serve several purposes. It will show that you really were listening, it will give both you and the student a chance to clarify anything that has been misunderstood or has been unclear and it will help you to remember what has been said so that you can make a record of the conversation once the student has left.

'I find a good way to wrap things up is to spend a minute or two summarizing what I've been told. Often it will initiate a bit more discussion as the student tries to clarify what they meant by something or to correct an assumption I've wrongly made so it's important to ensure you have enough time.'

Agree next steps

It's important that the student feels that their disclosure has not led to an isolated conversation, but rather that the wheels are in motion for support and change. For that reason it's helpful to agree some next steps with the student – these might simply be to reconvene later on, once you've had a chance to seek advice from another member of staff, or it might be for the student to tell their parents and report back to you by tomorrow lunchtime. It almost doesn't matter what the next steps are but the student needs to feel that you're on side, that some action will be taken and that they have an agreed time to check back in with you or another member of staff. If possible, agree the next steps with the student rather than imposing them on the student; you'll find the student will be far more engaged with this whole process if they feel that they're being actively consulted at every step.

Give the student information or helplines

In the short term, it can be very helpful to provide the student with web addresses or telephone numbers of places that they can access help outside school hours. This is important, as later in the day they may feel very guilty for having talked to you about their difficulties and this may fuel the desire to carry out unsafe behaviours. Providing the student with leaflets or similar information that can be shared with parents can also be helpful if they are planning to talk to their parents. It may be very difficult for the child to adequately explain their issues, but a well-written factsheet will give their parents some of the initial information they need. You might choose also to share a phone number or email address that parents can use to contact you once their child has talked to them if you are not going to be involved in this initial conversation.

Make a record

It's very important that you write a clear record of what you've discussed with the student and what's been agreed in terms of next steps; not only will this help you to clarify things in your own mind and act as a useful aide memoire when talking to other staff or the student's parents, it could also act as important evidence if it becomes necessary to refer the student to an external agency for therapy or other support. You should document every meeting you have with the child, even if you only make very brief notes, for this reason.

LEARNING TO TAKE AWAY FROM THIS CHAPTER

- When a student chooses to share their self-harm or eating disorder concerns with you, this is a big step that may have taken them days or weeks to make. They need to feel listened to, supported and in no way judged.

- The severity of a student's injuries is not proportional to their distress. You should not pass judgement about their injuries but just treat them as fact.

- If there is an urgent need for first aid, this should take priority over all other concerns.

- You should never promise a student that you'll keep their disclosure confidential. There are steps you can take to retain their trust without making this promise.

- Students will often be very reluctant to inform their parents about their difficulties and you may need to go to some effort to talk through the potential responses a student expects and explain why their parents might respond in this way and what is likely to happen next.

- It's important to follow up a disclosure with some form of agreed action so that the student feels that the wheels are in motion for support and change.

THINGS TO DO

- Familiarize yourself with your school's child protection o safeguarding policy so you know what the appropriate response and referral pathway is if a student confides in you about self-harm or an eating disorder.

- Keep accurate records of disclosures that students make as well as any follow-up conversations.

CHAPTER 9

Working with Parents

This chapter will enable you to:

- ensure that your first meeting with a student's parents runs smoothly

- sensitively inform parents about their child's difficulties via telephone if they are unable to meet face to face

- promote positive relationships with students' parents by handling difficult scenarios proactively and sympathetically

- support a student's recovery by forming a recovery team with the student at the heart.

Unless you suspect or are told that a student is being neglected or abused at home, it almost always make sense to inform parents as quickly as possible about a student's self-harming or eating-disordered behaviours. Where abuse or neglect are suspected, the school's child protection procedures must be followed alongside any support that is offered to the child for their self-harm or eating difficulties.

School policy (and common sense) usually dictate that parents must be informed about any issue which puts a child at risk – both self-harm and eating disorders clearly fall into this category. Where this becomes less clear cut is with older children. Some schools or colleges may not have clear guidance as to whether the parents of children aged over 16 or over 18 should be informed and this can leave you in a difficult situation. In the absence of clear guidance, I would suggest that it always makes a lot of sense to involve parents in a student's recovery where possible and that with older children this can be especially important, as they must make preparations for where they will draw support from for their difficulties when their time at school or college comes to an end.

Parents are often very supportive of their children and are able to provide a continuity of care outside of school hours including weekends and holidays. A child's best chance of recovery generally comes from having a united recovery team consisting of friends, family, the school and any treatment provider they may be working with.

The first meeting

It is common for the school to become aware of a child's self-harming or eating-disordered behaviours before a child's parents. Only about one in ten children talk first to their parents about these types of concerns, with the vast majority talking to a friend or a trusted adult outside their immediate family. Therefore the school can often have an important role in informing parents and initiating and facilitating meetings with parents. If you find yourself in this position, here is some guidance to help you ensure that your first meeting with parents runs as smoothly as possible:

Think about location

With the help of the student, decide where the meeting should be held – at school, in their home or on neutral territory. You should do whatever you think will make the student and their parents feel most comfortable and bear in mind that those parents who had unpleasant experiences of school themselves may not feel comfortable attending the school for meetings.

Consider who should attend

Talk to the student about whether they would like to be present from the start of the meeting. Some students will prefer you to have an initial discussion with their parents and allow them to join in once their parents have had a chance to digest the information and calm down if necessary. Other students will want to be present and be responsible for informing their parents with your support. Think carefully with the student about the best approach and ensure you have a back-up plan in case things don't go as expected – for example, if a student says they want to inform their parents themselves but feels too anxious at the last moment. In this instance you would want to have pre-agreed that you will step in and tell the parents; you would also hope to have pre-agreed exactly what you would tell the child's parents.

> 'I wanted to tell my parents myself but in a safe environment where I had the back-up of my teacher who already knew about my problems and had been so supportive. It was really hard, but it was good because she was able to back me up and fill in the gaps and I think my parents took it more seriously and responded more calmly than if I'd tried to tell them on my own at home.'

The student may also like to bring a friend along for support, though this is not always appropriate for the very initial meeting. In terms of school staff, it is generally sensible to have a couple of relevant members of staff present to help facilitate the meeting but it is important not to create a situation where either the student or their parents find things overbearing, so think carefully about who is attending and what their role in the meeting is.

Consider the room set-up
Try to make sure that the room set-up lends itself to open conversation – a round table, or no table at all, feels less intimidating to all involved than being pitched against each other across a large desk. Make sure the room is a comfortable temperature and that there will be absolutely no interruptions. Phones should be off and minds should be focused.

Make sure you have tea and tissues
Tea or water will give people something to hold and divert their attention to during the more difficult moments – also you're all likely to do a lot of talking so you may get thirsty. Tissues too are a must. This is likely to be a very emotionally charged meeting for all involved. That's okay as you'll all soon be working together to make things better.

> 'I always make sure that I'm fully stocked on tea, coffee, fruit teas and juice before difficult meetings. It helps to break the ice and makes it feel less like a formal school meeting and more like a friendly chat. It can also be helpful to have a break to make refreshments part way through longer meetings.'

Remain objective
When outlining the student's eating disorder or self-harming behaviours to their parents, try to explain it objectively. 'We think Jane may be suffering from anorexia… Anorexia is…' is better than emotionally charged statements, such as, 'We've been distraught with worry, the weight has been dropping off Jane and she just hasn't seemed happy for weeks.' At this time you need to convey the basic information in order to ensure parents are informed and ready to support. Your approach will be picked up on and mirrored by parents, so if you are calm, measured and practical in your approach, parents are more likely to respond similarly. However, if you are highly emotional and clearly distraught with worry then parents, in turn, are likely to panic.

'I have to mentally prepare myself for initial meetings with parents. They can be so emotionally charged. I see my key role as keeping it calm, focused and practical. However attached I am to the student and however upsetting I find it, I try to remain completely unemotional whilst being supportive. I have simple strategies to help me – if things are getting too tricky I offer people a time out and let them go for a walk. Another strategy is that if I suddenly find myself overcome with emotion I take a few moments to think about what colour I should redecorate my living room, just to refocus my mind and reduce the intensity of my feelings.'

Focus on practical steps

This is not the place or the time to dwell on *why* the student has developed self-harming behaviours or an eating disorder. Your job is not to look back, but to look forwards at the practical steps towards helping the student get better and specifically to think about how parents and school staff can work together to support the student at this time. The student may explore the reasons underlying their thoughts and behaviours with a counsellor or other one-to-one support.

Agree next steps

By the end of the meeting, everyone should be agreed about what the next steps are and who is responsible for them. This will probably involve the student and their parents visiting the family doctor and you might also like to arrange another meeting in a week or two to follow up.

Share your contact details and be available

Make sure that you give the student's parents your contact details and ensure that they feel welcome to use them. Let them know the best times and methods to contact you. They are likely to have questions after the meeting as they will have had a huge amount to take in and to come to terms with. They may also just need someone to talk to.

'I always write down my contact details and give them to parents but I also try to follow up in the next day or two with an email or call just to check if the parents have any questions for me and to make sure things are okay. You'd be surprised how few people feel confident enough to pick up the phone and call you, even when you've clearly said that it's fine for them to do so.'

Give them information to take away

Giving parents leaflets to take away can be very helpful. You will, no doubt, have made an effort to explain self-harm or eating disorders to them during the meeting, but the parents may not have taken a huge amount in. Being given some basic information to take away will enable them to learn a bit more about their son or daughter's difficulties. It can also be helpful to signpost useful websites or helplines. There is a lot of excellent support available but parents may not know where to find it or realize that there is support available for parents as well as sufferers. Visit www.inourhands.com/free-resources for a list of up-to-date resources.

> 'I found the leaflets reassuring as I'd found it hard to take everything in, so having some information I could read afterwards was helpful.'

Informing parents via telephone

It's always preferable to inform a parent of their child's eating disorder or self-harming behaviours in a face-to-face meeting where you can read and respond to body language. However, it's not always possible, for a whole host of reasons, so you may end up having to have the conversation on the phone. In this case the following points are worth bearing in mind:

Choose the most appropriate parent

Ask the student which of their parents would be better to speak to. They are likely to have a good idea about which of their parents is most likely to be supportive, understanding and comfortable discussing such a sensitive issue.

Plan what to say

Make a list of the points you want to cover beforehand – it can be very easy to become flustered on the phone if the conversation is difficult, or to fail to mention certain things if the conversation goes off in a different direction than you'd planned for. Having a checklist will make it easy to ensure you've covered all the points you need to before you end the call.

> 'I have a standardized list which I adapt to the specific parent and situation. It was borne out of necessity as so often I'd put the phone down then have to call back immediately because there was something really important I'd forgotten to say.'

TALKING TO PARENTS ON THE PHONE: CHECKLIST

When phoning a parent to inform them about their child's self-harming or eating-disordered behaviours, it can be helpful to have a checklist of things you want to remember to say. This list may be a useful starting point that you can adapt according to the situation.

- who you are – your role and why it's you making the call
- why you are concerned about the student
- basic information about self-harm or eating disorders
- reassurance that with support the student will be okay
- how you/the school intend to support in the short term
- advice about keeping their child safe in the short term
- arrange a time and place to meet face to face
- what help is available via school
- how the parent can help the child access support if appropriate
- sources of further information, such as websites and helplines
- provide your contact details and invite the parent to call back with questions.

Call at a good time

Pre-arrange a good time to call so that both you and the parent have time to talk. This is not a conversation that can be rushed.

> 'I always ask the student when is likely to be a good time to call and use that as a starting point. I also ask the student if they want me to call at a time when they will be at home so their parent can talk to them straight after the call or if they'd prefer to let their parents mull things over whilst they're at school.'

Focus on the call

Make the call from somewhere where you won't be distracted and which is free from background noise. Focus only on the call – concentrate on listening and responding to the parent as well as putting across the points you need to share.

Get to the point

Don't beat about the bush; the parent will want to know why you're calling and they won't hear anything you say until you get to the point of the call.

Ask how they feel about things

Invite the parent to share their concerns; they are likely to have suspected there was a problem, but may not have had a chance to talk about it before now.

Ask for their support

Make it clear that you're calling both to inform the parent about their child's difficulties and to ask for their help and support during their child's recovery.

Encourage questions

Give the parent plenty of space to explore their concerns or ask questions. It's okay to leave a few moments silence whilst they mull things over – they will need time to think as this is a lot of information to take in.

> 'I ask every few minutes "Do you have any questions?" because sometimes they feel too shy to speak up or ask otherwise. I always end the call by asking again if they've got any questions and giving them my number and email address so they can follow up. They usually have some questions later on once they've had a chance to think about things.'

Suggest a face-to-face meeting

If practicable, encourage them to meet you in person to discuss the issue further. Whilst they may not have been able to make it into school for this initial conversation, it is likely that they will want to meet face to face once they understand the gravity of the situation.

Dealing with difficult scenarios

Whilst most parents will be keen from the outset to support the school in helping their child receive appropriate support for their eating disorder or self-harming behaviours, some parents will give an initially negative response. It's important to overcome these negative responses so that we can move on and work together with parents to support the child in their recovery so I've outlined three of the most common negative responses school staff tend to encounter, along with suggestions for how you might counter these.

Responding to parents who think you're blaming them for their child's difficulties

If you put yourself in the shoes of a parent for a moment and imagine the scenario of learning that your son or daughter is suffering from self-harming or eating-disordered behaviours, not from your child but from their school, then it's easy to understand why a parent might feel guilty, upset or angry in the first instance.

Often the guilt that a parent feels about not being aware of their child's issues can result in an angry exchange where a parent accuses you of suggesting they are a bad parent or that they are to blame for their child's difficulties. This is often a result of the parent projecting their feelings on to you and reflects the fact that the parent does feel guilty and responsible, despite the fact that they have done nothing wrong.

> 'I've had quite a few parents shout at me and say that I was calling them a bad parent. When they feel that way, what they need most is support and guidance.'

At this point, your key role is to offer reassurance. However difficult the conversation it's important to stay calm, remain positive and keep the focus on the needs of the child. You can help to relieve the parent's concerns in the following ways:

- Reassuring them that 90 per cent of children choose not to tell a parent about self-harm or eating-disordered behaviour because they do not want to worry them. It is far easier for a student to make a disclosure to a trusted adult they care a little less for, such as someone at school or the parent of a friend.

- Making it clear that if you suspected that they were in any way responsible for their son or daughter's issues then you would not be calling them now. Instead, this would be being treated as a child protection issue and the appropriate authorities would be being involved. The fact you are having this discussion demonstrates that you in no way feel that they are to blame for their child's difficulties.

- Reiterating that you have called the parent so that they can work together with the school to support their son or daughter. Far from accusing them of bad parenting, you are seeking their help because you respect them as a good and supportive parent.

Useful phrases you could use include:

- No one is to blame for Amy's illness – not Amy, not us and not you.

- You are clearly very supportive parents, that's why we called you.

- Amy is very lucky to have supportive parents such as yourselves.

- We're not interested in attributing blame, we just want to help Amy get better and we're sure you can help.

Responding to parents who think you're blowing up the problem out of proportion

Some parents will minimize the problem or refuse to accept that there is an issue at all. In this instance you need to explain exactly what is causing your concern and why you think there is an issue. Parents who react like this are sometimes unaware of the existence of eating disorders or may think that self-harm is an attention-seeking behaviour. You may need to help them learn more about their child's difficulties and about the potential ramifications.

> 'His mum said she already knew about his self-harm but it didn't really worry her because it was something that most teenagers did and he'd just grow out of it.'

> 'I got the distinct impression from early on in the call that eating disorders were something he was previously unaware of. He dismissed my concerns because he didn't understand how serious this could get if we didn't act quickly. Whilst I didn't want to alarm him unduly, I did find it necessary to explain a bit about eating disorders and how harmful they could be, followed by some suggestions for how we could prevent his daughter's condition from worsening. Once he understood the seriousness of the situation he was very happy to help.'

Useful phrases you could use include:

- You're right, not everyone who goes on a diet has an eating disorder, but in James's case there are certain warning signs that tell us he's taken things too far.

- James may be in the very early stages of an eating disorder but he is far more likely to recover completely and be able to get on with his schoolwork and his life if we address his problems early.

- The reason we're worried about Cecily is because we've noticed that…

In situations where you find it hard to get parents to take their child's self-harming or eating-disordered behaviours seriously face to face or over the phone despite your best efforts, a tactic I have found to have great success is to write a letter to the parents, on school letter-headed paper, outlining the evidence underlying your concerns about their child and inviting them to meet with you. A formal letter of this type often seems to make parents realize that you are very concerned about their child and that you need their support to move forwards.

In some extreme cases, where parents absolutely refuse to acknowledge a problem, and their lack of support has the potential to do harm to their child because it is not possible to make an appropriate referral without their consent, then the issue becomes one of child protection and should be pursued according to your school's child protection or safeguarding policies. However, this is not a decision to be taken lightly, as this is an action that may secure the treatment that a child needs, but is likely to destroy any potential for a positive and supportive relationship between the parents and the school. This relationship can be key to recovery so if at all possible it is worth attempting to address your concerns through an alternative route.

> 'It was with heavy hearts that we involved social services. We knew that in some ways we would do more harm than good. However, we had a duty of care to the student and could not stand by and watch things get any worse. She was rapidly admitted for inpatient care and is now well on the road to recovery.'

Responding to parents who don't think the school should be involved
Occasionally a parent will feel that their child's difficulties are beyond the school's remit and should be dealt with solely at home. In these situations you need to explain how the school will be able to offer support and guidance and discuss with them, on a basic level, that as the child spends half their waking hours in school, the school does need to be involved, as their child's difficulties will be present for 24 hours a day.

> 'It was quite simple in the end – I just pointed out that however good a job was being done at home, their daughter was with us for six hours or more each day and that if they didn't talk to us we wouldn't be in a position to help. I don't think they'd thought about it from that point of view before.'

'It became apparent, via another student, that he was telling his parents that he was eating at school, which meant that they were more lenient about his meals at home. Of course he was not eating at school – but when quizzed he told staff he'd eaten breakfast before school and would have tea when he arrived home. Once we realized what was going on, the parents accepted that we absolutely needed to work together if we were to help their son recover.'

Useful phrases you could use include:

- We're keen to work with you and support you – we really think we can help.

- If we all work together to support Sandra, she is far more likely to get better.

- We're not trying to tell you how to care for your daughter, we simply want to offer our support.

Some parents will attempt to keep their child's difficulties secret from the school, due to concerns that their child will be bullied or discriminated against if their peers or teachers become aware that they are receiving treatment for a mental health or emotional wellbeing issue. It's important to make it clear to parents that the school is fully supportive and that the child will be judged neither at school nor during college or university application processes based on their mental or emotional health. This can be a major concern to parents.

Supporting recovery using a recovery team and a person-centred approach

A wide range of different people may become involved in the student's recovery including the student, their friends and parents, school staff and external agencies such as a counsellor or a mental health worker. It's advisable to have everyone work together as one team, with the aim of offering help and support to the student during recovery. The most important job of this team is to empower the student in question to make steps towards their own recovery and enable them to embrace the daily challenges this will bring.

In order for a student to make a sustainable recovery, they have to drive the process. This may mean things move a little more slowly or that there is some discussion over recovery priorities, but there is no doubt that a fuller and longer-lasting recovery will be made by a student who feels in control and at the centre of the process.

KEY POINTERS FOR HELPING THE STUDENT FEEL IN CONTROL

Don't

- talk about them as if they're not in the room (this is very easy to do)

- dismiss their point of view even if you don't feel it's valid

- underestimate how difficult this is for them

- arrange meetings without checking the location/timing works for them.

Do

- involve them in forming the recovery team

- ensure they are involved in discussions about their recovery

- discuss things using language that is accessible to them

- talk to them about how they'd like the room set up for meetings

- let them set the agenda (however informally) where possible. They will often want to discuss highly practical issues such as where they should eat their meals and with whom, whether they are allowed to participate in sport and who to talk to if they're having a difficult day

- offer continuous but unobtrusive support beyond meetings by making yourself available to them but never singling them out in front of their peers

- take time to praise them for their progress and involvement.

Working as a team and setting goals

There are no hard and fast rules about how often everyone should meet as a team in order to offer a student effective support and you should let the student drive this where possible, and expect the frequency and length of meetings to change throughout the recovery journey. It is useful to have at least one initial meeting with everyone involved in the student's recovery. This meeting should entirely revolve around the student, their needs, their recovery goals and how the team can support this.

With support, encourage the student to discuss what they are currently finding difficult and what their goals are. The team's job is to determine how to help the student overcome these difficulties and support team-agreed goals.

The meeting should have an informal atmosphere in which everyone feels able to put forward their point of view. Make it clear that the meeting is entirely confidential. It can be useful, at first, to have fairly frequent follow-up meetings with smaller groups to ensure progress and tackle any difficulties as they arise. The only person who must be offered the opportunity to attend every time is the student.

RECOVERY GOALS

One of the team's roles is to help the student work towards recovery goals. These should be determined by the student but agreed by the team as a whole. When goals are first set, it is very helpful to have present anyone formally involved in the recovery, for example, a psychiatrist, educational psychologist or counsellor, as they'll be able to offer useful direction and focus.

The focus should be on social and emotional goals rather than food, weight goals or harm reduction goals. (These last three should be tackled by the student with their psychiatrist, counsellor or trusted adult they are working with at home or school.)

The goals can be quite simple and should each help address something the student is currently struggling with at school. They might include things such as:

- to come to school every day for a week

- to spend time with friends at break time

- to contribute to class discussion.

The goals should be achievable with the help of the team and everyone should give suggestions as to how they can support the student with each of their goals whilst ensuring the student gets the opportunity to share their thoughts about what they think would be most helpful.

LEARNING TO TAKE AWAY FROM THIS CHAPTER

- It is worth investing time, effort and energy to ensure that initial conversations with parents are positive. If the school is able to work effectively with parents, the student's chance of a rapid and full recovery is greatly increased.

- Parents will sometimes respond negatively when informed about their child's difficulties. This is usually short-lived if you respond sensitively and supportively.

- A person-centred approach to recovery with the student at the heart of a practically focused recovery team can help the student to feel more in control of their own recovery, increasing the chance of success as the student is more motivated.

- It's important to work with the student to set recovery goals. These should be simple and practical and every member of the recovery team should think about how they can support the student in achieving these goals.

THINGS TO DO

- Create a checklist of things you need to remember to mention when having initial conversations with parents about their child's difficulties to ensure nothing goes forgotten.

- Think about how you can apply some of what you have learned whilst reading this chapter to improve any more difficult relationships you currently have with students' parents.

- Reflect on any difficult scenarios you've encountered in the past when working with parents and think about how you might handle a similar situation differently in future.

- Consider whether any of the students currently in your care would benefit from moving towards a more student-centred approach and/or the use of a focused recovery team.

CHAPTER 10

When and How to Refer a Student for Specialized Support

This chapter will enable you to:

- understand when it is and when it is not appropriate or necessary to seek the support of an external agency such as the Child and Adolescent Mental Health Services (CAMHS)

- understand how to make a referral to CAMHS

- write effective high-quality referrals which are more likely to result in a prompt response from CAMHS

- phone CAMHS to express your concerns and inform them that you are sending in a referral

- develop positive relationships with external agencies

- effectively support students who are receiving external support.

When is specialist support needed?

When a student is facing mental health or emotional wellbeing issues, our first thought is often 'Where can we refer them?' because we assume that supporting them is beyond the capabilities of school staff. However, this is not always the case and in some instances there are strong arguments for providing support at school. In most cases, the student and their family are well-known to school staff, which will better enable them to help, and more long-term support is likely to be possible – whereas many referrals to external agencies will result in a strictly finite course of therapy or similar help. In addition to this, ever-shrinking budgets mean that the amount of external support available is strictly limited and that, where it is possible to access support, this help may come only after a wait of several weeks or even months.

In some cases, specialist help is needed and students will be fast-tracked for support, though even this does not guarantee there will be no wait at all. In particular, students who are found to be suffering from severe eating disorders, especially if they are very underweight, may be fast-tracked for treatment, as will students who are contemplating suicide. If a student's condition results in an emergency hospital visit, then in many instances they will not be discharged without first seeing a member of the child and adolescent mental health team. Whilst this will not guarantee a referral for treatment, it often speeds things up where a referral is clearly needed.

Before referring a student for external support, you should consider carefully whether this support is needed and whether your referral is likely to be successful. In many instances, students can be effectively supported through their difficulties by staff at school, especially where they have access to a counsellor or school staff who have experience of supporting students in similar situations. However, there are some situations in which a referral is always warranted.

A student should always be referred for specialist support in these situations

- You think the student may have suicidal feelings.

- They have attempted suicide or talked about a suicide plan.

- Their self-harm is so severe that it is putting their physical health in danger.

- You think they may have a diagnosable eating disorder.

- Symptoms have developed very rapidly and the situation is not stabilizing.

- The student has been, or is being, neglected or abused.

- You think the difficulties were triggered by a significant trauma that the child may need help in coming to terms with (e.g. rape, witnessing the death of a loved one, etc.).

- You think the student poses a significant risk to themselves or others by remaining in school.

- You have attempted to support the student at school but have tried all interventions available to you and the situation is not improving/ has got worse.

CHOOSING A PRIVATE PROVIDER OF SPECIALIST HEALTHCARE

In some instances it may be more appropriate to refer a student to private specialist services rather than CAMHS. This is likely to result in a far quicker turnaround with minimal waiting times, but this can prove to be very costly for the family even if they have health insurance to cover such costs, as treatment will often exceed the maximum amount that insurers are happy to contribute, especially if the child's difficulties are very severe or enduring. This, and the need to carefully vet any potential services, should be borne in mind and discussed with parents when considering a referral.

In order to identify whether the service is likely to meet the needs of their child, parents can:

- talk to existing service users/their families about their experiences

- ask the provider whether they are in any way accredited and ask for details of what treatment will be provided and by whom – and what their qualifications are

- visit the service and consider whether it seems like somewhere their child would feel safe and supported

- ask staff for typical duration and cost of treatment for students in a similar situation to their son/daughter

- ask staff about relapse rates and how relapses are managed.

Mental health and other specialist charities will often hold a list of approved private providers or may be able to put parents in touch with other parents in the local area who have had positive (or negative) experiences with particular services that they are happy to share. This is worth exploring. Whilst the need to embark on treatment can seem very pressing, the need to source the right support is more so; it is absolutely worth taking a little time to do some due diligence before a child embarks on private treatment.

How the referral process works

The process for referring to your local Child and Adolescent Mental Health Services (CAMHS) varies geographically. In some instances, school staff, school nurses or parents are able to refer directly, in other cases referrals must be made via a student's doctor. Depending on the age of the child, parental consent may be required for a referral – it makes a lot of sense to be working with parents where possible in any case, regardless of the age of the child.

Some CAMHS teams have very specific referral processes which require a detailed form to be completed outlining the student's needs and difficulties, other CAMHS simply require a referral letter or phone call – in either case, there are clear steps you can take to increase the chances of a successful referral.

How to increase the likelihood of a successful CAMHS referral

Decreasing budgets and an increasing number of cases of self-harm and eating disorders mean that schools are finding it increasingly difficult to successfully refer children to child and adolescent mental health services. In order to maximize the chances of a successful referral there are some simple steps you can follow:

Ensure that a referral is needed

Try only to make a referral where one is genuinely needed and it is not possible for the school to provide adequate support to the student without external intervention. You may sometimes be unsure about whether or not it is appropriate or necessary to make a referral. In these instances it can be helpful to have an initial conversation with someone from CAMHS who will be able to give you a good steer on whether they feel a referral is needed at this time.

Write a full and thorough referral

You should approach referral writing like an exam. There is a mark scheme – the more boxes you can tick that suggest your support is needed, the more likely you are to succeed in accessing support. If you're completing a form provided by CAMHS, don't leave any gaps; take the time you need to gather any supplementary information. If you're writing a free-form referral, useful information to include is:

- student details
- parent/carer contact details
- supporting statement
- relevant records/reports

- contact details for lead at school

- support already offered by the school.

Many people write referrals hurriedly because of the many time pressures they face at school, but saving time on referral writing is a false economy. CAMHS only know as much information about a student as you provide, and bearing in mind the stiff competition for referrals in the current climate you need to make your case as comprehensively as possible. Faced with two students struggling with similar difficulties, one with a brief or incomplete referral and one with a detailed, thorough referral, CAMHS are likely to work first with the more complete referral as it is likely that a more compelling case will have been made.

Think carefully when providing contact details
Even relatively simple parts of the referral process need a little thought and attention. For example, when providing contact details for yourself, or the relevant person at school with whom CAMHS should be in touch with regard to the referral, think carefully about the best contact details to provide. School staff are notoriously difficult to get hold of due to the many calls on their time; providing the telephone number for an office you rarely get time to sit in is not the best call of action. Instead, think about providing a mobile number or email address and/or specifying particular times at which you are most likely to be available. If CAMHS want to follow up on a referral but are completely unable to contact you, they are likely to eventually move on to the next student on their long waiting list.

Demonstrate the day-to-day impact of the child's difficulties
When making your referral you should think carefully about what evidence you can provide about how the student's difficulties are negatively impacting on their day-to-day life. This may include both academic and social factors. Relatively easy factors to evidence are more frequent absenteeism or a drop in attainment as shown by their student records. You might also consider less tangible factors, like observations that the student has become increasingly isolated and finds it difficult to interact with their peers, or has dropped out of extracurricular activities that they previously found great pleasure in. Basically, have a think about what in the student's day-to-day life has changed as a result of their difficulties and how this can be evidenced. Consider also over what time period these changes have occurred and whether they are getting worse – if so, how can you prove this? If you are able to demonstrate to

CAMHS that the students' self-harming or eating difficulties are having a significant and sustained impact on their day-to-day life then your referral will be taken very seriously.

Outline ways in which the school has already tried to help
The job of CAMHS is to provide specialist support where it is not possible for a student to be supported by non-specialists, including school staff. So, before a referral can be made, unless the situation is urgent, CAMHS will be asking what the school has already done to help and what impact this has had. You should provide details of any interventions that you've put in place with the child – these do not have to be incredibly formal procedures; the fact that Amy has been sitting down for half an hour twice a week with Mrs Gibbs for a chat is absolutely the kind of thing that you should be telling CAMHS. Try to provide evidence for the impact, or otherwise, that your interventions have had. CAMHS help is most needed where the school has tried several different methods of intervention with a student but the situation is not stabilizing or is actively getting worse. Being able to prove this is the case will add strength to your referral.

Getting the child's doctor on board

Whilst it is not always necessary to make a referral to CAMHS via the student's doctor, many people find that this speeds up the referral process, as a referral that comes from a doctor or that is jointly signed by a doctor will carry a lot of weight. The most common strategy for getting the student's doctor on board is to ask the student and their parent to visit the doctor. In this situation it is advisable to provide a letter to the doctor, perhaps sent ahead of the appointment, to be shared at the appointment by the student and their parent. In this letter you can provide information about the student and their difficulties and fill in any gaps that you fear may not get covered in a short appointment slot. Working with the child's doctor is probably the best approach for ensuring a successful referral as you will have a lot more information about the child's history and the impact of their difficulties, so in your letter encourage the doctor to get in touch with you to discuss the case so you can make a joint referral, or you can provide any additional information needed for the doctor to make a referral.

Developing a positive relationship with external agencies

If you are successful in making a referral to CAMHS or another external agency, it is worth investing some time and effort in building a positive relationship with the staff responsible for your student's care. This will enable you and the external agency to provide better care to the child in question, who will benefit from a collaborative and consistent approach, and it will also put you in a better position next time you need support from CAMHS as you will no longer be a stranger to the relevant staff and team.

Work on building the relationship with CAMHS – get to know them by suggesting a meeting about the child; parents may also attend this. Make it easy for the CAMHS staff by suggesting that you visit them instead of expecting them to come to school. Seek their advice and respect their professional opinion when it comes to knowing how best to support the student and be sure to show your appreciation of any support you or the student receive. CAMHS are very used to receiving criticism but few people take the time to say thank you for what is often an excellent service. Taking a moment to show your appreciation will set you apart from 99 per cent of the people that CAMHS deal with.

In the UK, in some geographic areas there are local meetings such as multi-agency forums (MAFs) where school staff can meet with other professionals to share information and gain understanding of how each agency works – including thresholds of interventions. This is worth exploring. There are also many benefits to making use of the Common Assessment Framework (CAF), a shared assessment and planning framework for use across all children's services and all local areas in England. It aims to help the early identification of children and young people's additional needs and promote co-ordinated service provision to meet them.

Supporting a child whilst they are receiving external support

If a child is referred for specialist support, this does not mean that there is no role for the school to play. First, there may be a waiting list, so it is important for the school to help the child manage their situation until their treatment commences, and, second, both the school and the child's parents have important roles to play in supporting and reinforcing the messages conveyed and behaviours encouraged as a result of any treatment. In many cases treatment is minimal, typically an hour or two a week, so it is vital that the child receives support outside their specified treatment sessions. Additionally, treatment duration is often strictly limited. Many students will be treated until they are out of serious danger both physically and mentally, and then they may be discharged. Arguably this is the point at which the hard work really starts and, again, there is much that can be done by the school and the family.

The ideas shared later in this book about supporting children in recovery can also be used alongside treatment by an external agency such as CAMHS. You can also ask the child's care provider if they have any guidance or specific ideas about how you can best support them. They may or may not offer guidance, but it is important, where possible, that you become aware of the general direction of treatment and any key messages that need to be reinforced. You may learn these directly from the care provider or from the child or their parents. Where this information is not available for whatever reason, providing general support will be more helpful than harmful and will prevent the child from feeling overly anxious as their treatment cycle comes to an end.

LEARNING TO TAKE AWAY FROM THIS CHAPTER

- There is a lot that schools can do to support students with less severe difficulties that may not warrant a CAMHS referral.

- However, there are some instances in which a referral should always be made.

- There is also a lot that schools can do to support students whilst they receive external treatment.

- Writing full and thorough referrals outlining the key information required by CAMHS can increase the likelihood of a successful and rapid referral.

- There are private treatment alternatives available. These can prove costly and need to be considered carefully by the student and their family.

THINGS TO DO

- Learn about your local CAMHS referral processes so that you have all the information you need next time you need to make a referral.

- Discuss guidelines with other school staff about when referrals should be made and when cases should be handled at school. Most schools have a designated safeguarding lead who should be informed of or involved in the referral process.

- Identify relevant staff members at your local CAMHS team and think about how you can develop your relationship with them and draw on their expertise when needed.

CHAPTER 11

Supporting Students Who Require Inpatient Care

This chapter will enable you to:

- work with external agencies to provide appropriate support to students receiving inpatient care for self-harming or eating-disordered behaviours

- sensitively and supportively reintegrate students back into school following absence due to inpatient care

- prepare staff and students for a child's return to school

- understand and respond to warning signs that a student in recovery is heading towards a relapse.

Working with external agencies

If a student is particularly unwell, their healthcare practitioners may decide that inpatient care at a paediatric, psychiatric or eating disorders unit is the best treatment option for them. It's important for the school to remain informed about the student's recovery and to support as appropriate.

The school should appoint a key person who is responsible for liaising with the unit where the child is resident. This should be someone who is trained and experienced in dealing with child protection and safeguarding issues; it is not a suitable role for a newer member of staff unless thorough training is provided. The member of staff should make sure they have the full contact details of the key person who is assigned to the child's care at the unit and make themselves known. Arrange a meeting if possible, and if not then speak on the phone. The aim of the meeting is to clarify:

- who the main point of contact is at the school and how to get hold of them

- that the school is keen to support the child's recovery in any way possible – ask for guidance on this

- that the school is happy to co-ordinate the provision and marking of academic work if appropriate

- that the school would like regular updates about the child's recovery

- that the school would like to know what it is appropriate to tell staff and students about the student's absence

- that the school would like the child to know you called and that you/staff/friends are thinking of them.

Don't be afraid to ask for updates

Inpatient units are very busy places – it can be difficult for staff to keep on top of requests for regular updates about a particular patient, especially if these do not come from parents. Of course, the staff all want what is best for the patient and are likely to be very helpful if you call to enquire about their progress, so it's okay to pick up the phone. Sometimes persistence is the only way to gain the information that you need.

Providing academic work

The school should be prepared to provide and mark academic work if this is deemed appropriate by the unit. Alternatively, the school may be asked to liaise with an onsite education team to discuss the student's academic background and progress so that the onsite team can provide appropriate schooling. Of course, during a stay at an inpatient unit, the main focus is on restoring health and not on academics so it is to be expected that the student will not make the usual expected academic progress. However, some effort is often made to keep students up to speed with their peers where possible to lessen the difficulty of reintegration into school when the time is right.

Contact with friends

Depending on the severity of the student's illness and the general approach taken by the unit, the amount of contact allowed with friends could vary greatly. Many units will remove access to mobile phones and the internet during the most intense period of recovery – but they are still likely to welcome letters and cards from friends at school. If visiting or phone calls are allowed, you should encourage students to maintain contact with their friend if they feel comfortable doing so. If students are sending cards, letters or emails to their friend in an inpatient unit, please encourage them to continue doing so for the duration of their friend's stay. They may not receive any replies, but in almost all instances, cards, letters and other contact will be gratefully received by patients, even if they feel unable to formulate a reply. If for any reason the contact is upsetting or inappropriate then the staff at the unit will let you know.

Maintaining contact with the unit during recovery

Following discharge, if the student's care still officially falls under the unit, then it is helpful if you are able to stay in regular contact with the staff there. This can help you to tackle any difficult issues that arise during recovery and prevent a significant relapse. If the student's care is to be passed to an alternative care provider then you should try to arrange a meeting/telephone call with them so that they can support you in supporting the student during recovery.

Reintegrating students into school following inpatient treatment

Returning to school can be a cause of great fear and concern for students who have been in inpatient care, especially if they have been absent for some time. Handled incorrectly, the return to school can often trigger a relapse in emotions and behaviour severe enough to result in the student being readmitted to the unit they have recently left. School can be a great source of tension and stress for students in recovery and sometimes their eating disorder or self-harm may have been triggered by issues they faced at school but had been able to avoid at the inpatient unit. However, handled carefully and at the right pace, the return to school can be a very positive step for a student in recovery. They may be motivated and affirmed by their capacity to overcome this obstacle and empowered by their ability to continue their recovery in the 'outside world'.

Opting for a phased return to school

A phased return to school can be a less daunting alternative for a student than going immediately from being a full-time inpatient to a full-time student overnight. By working with staff at the unit as well as the student and their parents, you can agree a schedule for a phased return over a few weeks. This might start with the student having increased access to school staff and friends at the unit, followed by a visit to school for a few hours. You might then work towards them returning to school on a part-time timetable and eventually attending full time. Remember, it is better to take things slowly and at a pace that is manageable for the student rather than to try and rush things and risk ending up back at square one.

Considering academic expectations

It's important to think carefully about what the academic expectations are for a student, particularly where a significant period of school has been missed. Some people find that it is necessary, and indeed helpful, to drop back an academic year enabling a student to retake their classes and/or exams. This has the complication of meaning that the student needs to re-establish themselves amongst new peers, but for some students this is welcomed as the opportunity for a fresh start. This needs careful consideration by the school, the student and their parents and care must be taken to ensure that it is not seen as a sign of failure, which is how a student will often interpret it. It is important to explore these feelings with the student, which will often go unspoken but may otherwise play out in negative behaviours or a recurrence of their original self-harming behaviours or eating difficulties.

If it is considered unnecessary or inappropriate for the student to move down an entire academic year, an alternative is to consider whether they should have a reduced timetable. If they are working towards exams it may be appropriate for them to study fewer subjects than they'd originally intended to in order to give them time to catch up with and succeed in their remaining subjects. Again, students can be very resistant to this, feeling that it is important that they sit all of their exams in order to progress in their academic career. A useful approach to this predicament is to spend some time with the student and their parents considering the potential pathways that they intend to pursue following their upcoming exams and finding out what the specific entry criteria are for the student to be able to pursue their intended aims. It is often the case that a student is studying more subjects than are required by the institution they wish to move on to and it is also often true that fewer subjects performed at a higher level will stand them in better stead than having a broader range of exams completed to a lower level. It is also important to bear in mind the possibility of retaking examinations, if for any reason the student is unable to sit them or wishes to attempt to try for a better grade once they are further down the road of recovery.

When considering what academic expectations are realistic for a student, it's important to bear in mind the student's hopes and wishes as well as the views of their teachers and parents. Where possible, a student needs to feel in control, rather than penalized, during the process of recovery so if a student absolutely refuses to compromise on their academic endeavours then you should consider ways to support them to attempt a full timetable. You should also make sure it is possible for them to bow out gracefully from any subjects which ultimately do prove to be more than they can manage at this time, and remind them of the possibility of returning to them at a later date if this is what they wish to do.

Another way to relieve the pressure on students academically is to consider the other expectations that are currently placed on them. Perhaps they have a student leadership role or are involved in several extracurricular activities to a high level. Removing some of these pressures may help them to find time to catch up with their studies. However, it important that the student also finds ways to unwind and relax, though this may be better achieved through lower-pressure, uncompetitive extracurricular activities or simply through spending unstructured time with friends.

Identifying triggers

It is worth working with returning students to identify any specific triggers which they are concerned about facing on their return to school. This work may be sensitively done by the caregivers at their inpatient unit, or as part of your work with the student to prepare them for their return to school. Ideally you should have identified potential triggers and considered ways of avoiding or addressing them prior to the student's return.

There are a wide range of different things that might trigger negative thoughts and feelings in students; some are easier to address than others. For example, many students recovering from an eating disorder will be very fearful of eating in the school's canteen. This can be easily addressed by allowing them to eat their lunch elsewhere and developing a plan for gradually enabling them to eat lunch with their peers. Other common concerns include:

- bullying, teasing or upsetting use of language (e.g. 'mental' used as a slang term)

- participating in sports or physical education lessons

- changing in front of others

- speaking in front of the class

- having to be in the company of certain friends/teachers

- not keeping up academically

- sitting tests or exams.

Every student will have a slightly different set of anxieties about their return to school. You need to take care not to dismiss or belittle them; instead for each issue the student raises you should consider whether it can/should be avoided, adjusted or addressed in order to enable the student to feel more at ease about their return to school. Work with the student and their parents to come up with ideas and write a basic plan. Revisit this within the student's first day back to assess whether your initiatives are working or if further action is necessary. Continue to revisit it over the coming days and weeks to ensure that the student is as fully supported as possible during their transition back into school.

Understanding relapse warning signs

Relapse is a part of recovery and learning to recognize and manage the warning signs as early and as effectively as possible is an important skill for students in recovery to develop. It's helpful if you can be aware of the signs to look out for and know the most appropriate way to support the student should you spot these signs. Following a stay in an inpatient unit, students can often return to school armed with a range of strategies for better hiding their difficulties than they had prior to their treatment. This can make relapses hard to spot so you need to be very alert. During good patches, work with the student to identify likely triggers and the sorts of signs you might be able to spot. These might be physical or emotional – and many of them will be identical to the initial warning signs that indicate a student may be struggling with self-harming or eating-disordered behaviour explored earlier in this book. During positive periods of recovery, work with the student to identify what was more and less helpful in terms of responding to their difficulties in the past. This will enable you to provide the most helpful response to any future difficulties.

Peer support

Identifying a friend or two who can be closely involved in the student's reintegration can be a real support and is something that friends will often actively engage in as they tend to find themselves in a position where they want to help their friend but don't know how, or they're scared of getting things wrong and making things worse.

When implementing peer supporters it's important to consider:

- Who will support the peer supporters?

- What are the boundaries?

- When and how should peer supporters seek additional advice or help?

- What information is the young person comfortable with you sharing with their friend?

QUESTIONS TO ASK THE INPATIENT UNIT PRIOR TO THE STUDENT'S RETURN TO SCHOOL

There is a lot of information that can be usefully shared with the school by the unit prior to the student's return. This may not automatically happen so you need to be prepared to ask.

Key questions you can ask are:

- Does the student have a meal plan?

- How best can the school support the student during mealtimes?

- How much sport/exercise should the student be allowed to undertake?

- What (if any) academic progress has the student made whilst in the unit?

- What should the school do if they are worried the student might be relapsing?

- Can the school retain regular contact with the unit for advice/updates?

- Who is responsible for the student's care after discharge? Can they be put in touch with the school?

- Will the student be attending outpatient appointments, and how will this affect their school routine?

- Is there anything else the school needs to be aware of?

- What information is appropriate to share with staff and peers?

Preparing staff and peers for the student's return to school

There can be many questions surrounding a student's return to school following a period of absence. You cannot ignore the significance of this event and it is far better to think ahead and prepare staff and students by giving them an opportunity to explore their thoughts and questions prior to the student's return. You should be able to seek some guidance from staff at the unit about what information it is appropriate to share with staff and peers.

The guidelines shared earlier in this book about teaching students about self-harm and eating disorders should be adhered to when discussing these concerns with students prior to a peer's return, whether these discussions are a formal part of learning or more ad hoc.

LEARNING TO TAKE AWAY FROM THIS CHAPTER

- If a student's difficulties are especially severe or enduring, it may be considered appropriate for them to receive inpatient care.

- It is often possible for the school to provide some support to the student whilst they are resident at an inpatient unit. The unit will be able to direct you as to how best you can help.

- It is important to carefully consider how best to reintegrate a student into school following a period of inpatient care, as this can be a very vulnerable time.

- Identifying and managing triggers that may cause the student distress and being vigilant for relapse warning signs can help to improve the chances of a smoother recovery.

THINGS TO DO

- Consider what capacity the school has to support students when they are receiving inpatient care. Think about what might be optimal and what outline plans can be put in place ahead of any future cases.

- Think about the process for reintegrating students into school after an absence due to inpatient care. Sketch a rough plan of who might be involved and in what capacity, and whether there are any training or other needs that you should look to address in the medium term.

CHAPTER 12

Day-to-Day Strategies for Supporting Recovery at School

This chapter will enable you to:

- support students academically including in a classroom setting

- provide students with the support they need in the run-up to school holidays

- implement specific strategies for supporting students who self-harm

- implement specific strategies for supporting students with eating disorders

- support students during panic attacks.

General ideas for supporting students academically and in class

You could explore the various ideas outlined in this chapter with the student and their parents as part of your recovery team work. On the whole, you will see most success when the student plays a role in determining what sort of support and help is needed and how this might best be implemented.

Academic expectations

An important consideration when supporting any student who is currently suffering from or recovering from self-harm or an eating disorder is about ensuring that the school, the student and their parents all have realistic academic expectations. Expecting a child to achieve beyond what they are currently capable of due to their psychological or physical wellbeing or following a period of absence can result in the student failing to live up to their expectations, which can feed into their anxieties and harmful behaviours.

In order to keep things realistic for the student, you might like to consider:

- discussing grades with the student – should they be aiming for B grades instead of A grades?

- whether the student may require additional academic support or tutoring

- whether the student should be relieved of any additional responsibilities they hold, such as being a prefect, in order to relieve them of stress and to free up some time

- whether the student should drop some or all of their extracurricular activities to free up their time

- whether the student should drop a subject or two

- whether the student should restart the year.

Any decision about the student's academic trajectory needs to be taken with rather than for the student and their opinion needs to be carefully considered, even if it is not in line with your way of thinking.

Another strategy which many people find helpful is to discuss a homework time limit with parents as many students will stay up for many, many hours perfecting their homework at the cost of sleep (which is key to recovery). If the school, parents and student agree on a time limit for homework, for instance, two hours, then the parents can enforce this and the student will tend to respect it.

Response to failure

Self-harm and eating disorders sufferers will often define themselves more keenly in terms of success and failure than most people do. That means that you have to think very carefully about how you respond to failure – and remember that devastating failure for an eating disorder sufferer might be something as seemingly trivial as achieving a B grade. Look for the positives and try to find the success in failure. Learning to manage failure is a very important lesson for those trying to recover from eating disorders as, sadly, this is a path fraught with failure – both imagined (they will feel they've failed when they eat a healthy meal, although everyone else might see it as a huge success) and real (relapse is very common: recovery can be very two steps forwards, one step back).

We also need to think carefully about how we respond to academic success. By emphasizing academic achievements, we are inadvertently putting pressure on the student to succeed, which can feed into their difficulties. Where staff are aware that a student is struggling with an eating disorder, it is common for them to redouble their focus on academic achievement as something positive to talk about. This is something to be aware of, as it is actually far from positive for someone in the grip of an eating disorder to spend many hours each night obsessing over homework in order not to let their grade average slip.

Considering the curriculum

Care should be taken to consider the content of the curriculum of the subjects that any student in recovery is studying. If possible they should not be put in a position where they are made to feel uncomfortable or their unhealthy coping mechanisms triggered by lesson content. Sometimes this can be quite obvious – for example if your scheme of work contained an eating disorders module – other times it might be a little less so, such as maths lessons which considered weight and numbers or biology or food technology lessons which considered digestion or healthy eating.

Where there is concern that lesson content may be difficult for a student in recovery, then the lesson should be discussed with them beforehand, either by the teacher or, preferably, by the school counsellor or other trusted adult the student is having regular meetings with. Allowing the student to review the lesson material ahead of the lesson will enable them either to psychologically prepare themselves for the lesson or to opt out of the lesson. You might like to encourage the student to make any suggestions to slightly amend the lesson which might make them feel more comfortable. Simple things such as ensuring that all case studies refer to a male if the student is female and vice versa might distance the learning and help the student to feel a little more comfortable.

Free pass and bolt hole

Sometimes, despite your best efforts, a student will become unable to manage in a lesson. This may be because they find the content disturbing or triggering, or it may have nothing to do with the specific lesson but rather be to do with the student's frame of mind at that particular time.

If a student feels unable to manage in lessons, it is generally counter-productive to make them stay. This insistence is likely to cause a great deal of anxiety in the student and could result in a full-blown panic attack or a self-harming incident occurring in the classroom. Instead it is advisable to allow them to leave the lesson. Many schools now have a system in place where vulnerable students are provided with a 'free pass' to leave class. This can be given for a variety of reasons and enables the student to leave any lesson if they feel unable to manage, without the teacher leading the lesson questioning them.

Free passes are most effective if they are:

- *used sparingly* – class teachers are more likely to cooperate if the system is not open to abuse or overuse.

- *provided in physical form* – a small card that a child can carry around that states they have permission to leave class and is signed by a senior member of staff sends a clear message to the class teacher and can also provide great comfort to the student. Many students will treat this card like a security blanket. They may test it once or twice to ensure that it actually works; after that, many students will find simply knowing they could leave if they needed to has enough of a calming effect to enable them to remain in the lesson.

- *reviewed regularly* – free passes should have expiry dates on them and should be issued only for a few weeks at a time as a general rule. When the expiry date comes up, have a conversation with the student about whether they still need a free pass and do not hesitate to issue a new one if it is needed – even if the student appears not to be using it, as it may be quelling their anxiety.

'It was like that little card had magic powers for me. Just having it in my pocket made me feel okay. If I started to feel the panic rising I'd just put my hand in my pocket and feel my card there and then I would focus on my breathing and start to calm down. I only actually used it once.'

Students cannot simply leave a lesson when they are in a state of panic or heightened anxiety; it's important to have a designated 'bolt hole' for them to go to. At this point a student is at higher risk than usual of harming themselves or absenting themselves from school so where possible, they should be accompanied to a designated safe place. Alternatively, the class teacher may call ahead to the designated safe place so that the student is expected imminently and the alarm can be raised if they do not show up (this only works for low-risk students). The safe place or bolt hole should be somewhere where the student feels safe and comfortable. It needs to be somewhere that has a level of supervision to ensure the student does not self-harm and so that they have someone they can talk to if they feel the need to do so. Suitable places include the school library, a common room, a school nurse's or designated member of school staff's office or an internal exclusion centre/time out room/cooler.

As well as having a plan for where the student will go, it is also helpful to have a plan of what they will do. Any activity which will help them to calm down is preferable and, as they are unlikely to be able to think coherently whilst in a heightened state of panic, it is helpful to have a pre-agreed plan with the student about what they will do in order to calm down. What works best will depend on the student but activities which students commonly find useful in this situation are:

- reading
- listening to music
- drawing
- writing
- doing homework.

Essentially, they should be activities which enable the student to calm down and focus on something other than what is worrying them.

> 'I had this special colouring book. It was designed to calm you down. It wasn't like a kids' colouring book, it had all these beautiful patterns in it. Some were quite complicated. As I sat colouring, I would feel myself get calmer.'

Regular access to a trusted adult

Students find having regular access to a trusted adult both helpful and reassuring. There are two different key purposes that such an adult or adults can serve. First, they can offer support and guidance with regard to academic and more general issues; second, they can offer more therapeutic and counselling-type support. These two roles may be fulfilled by the same person or by two different people.

The first type of support is highly practical and enables a student to highlight any issues they are coming up against in their day-to-day life at school, both within and beyond lessons. Being able to talk these issues through and seek reassurance from a trusted adult can be both reassuring and helpful to a student in recovery and can be a useful forum for seeking solutions where they are needed. The second type of support is more specialized – where a member of staff takes on a counselling-type role. Ideas for providing this type of support effectively are provided later on in this book.

The most appropriate frequency and duration of meetings with a trusted adult will vary from student to student and over time. We can be guilty of assuming a 'one size fits all' mentality when approaching these issues and assuming that because the last student we worked with thrived on twice-weekly meetings that lasted half an hour, this will be the right answer for the student we've just started seeing. Some students find very frequent meetings to be reassuring, though these may be very short. They may be as frequent as three times a day, but could last no more than five minutes at a time. Some students are content even just to write a note to the member of staff they're seeing, just to say they're okay. On the other hand, some students do not feel the need for frequent catch-ups, but they would prefer to sit down for 40 minutes or more at a time. This might be as infrequently as once a week or once a fortnight. A student's preferences with regard to meeting frequency and duration are likely to change over time, so it is worth revisiting this periodically to ensure that you are supporting in the most effective way you can. In the run-up to school holidays, it is also worth considering whether it is possible to wean students off contact time if they are having very regular or very long meetings in order to prepare them for periods away from school.

> 'At first I needed constant reassurance and it would be three or four times a day that we would talk, with one longer meeting at the beginning of the week. As the weeks went by, I became less anxious and we dropped all of the meetings except the one long one. I needed that one for quite a long time. It was during those meetings that we talked about coping strategies and ways for me to move on with a new way of life rather than reverting to bingeing again.'

There is a wide range of staff who may fulfil these roles, ranging from form tutors to house parents to sports coaches or school nurses. The student will often gravitate towards a particular member of staff as someone they trust and feel comfortable talking to. If this is not a member of staff who has experience or expertise in counselling and supporting students in this way then they should be provided with training where possible and should always be able to rely upon the supervision and support of a mentor. Whilst any member of staff who is happy to do so may take on the role of trusted adult, ally and supportive listener, more specialist help should only be provided by trained staff who hold professional indemnity insurance or are covered for such work by the school.

STUDENTS IN RECOVERY: BEING HELPFUL IN CLASS

Many teachers can feel so worried about saying or doing the wrong thing that they end up almost avoiding students known to be recovering from self-harm or eating disorders. What these students really need is to feel supported, included, valued and treated like 'normal' members of the class, as these students in recovery have demonstrated.

'My biology teacher said, "How can I support you in my lessons?" and he took the time to listen to the answers and support me as I asked. That was fantastic.'

'I'd alienated my friends, so in group work there was no one to work with really. One teacher noticed and, instead of letting us pick our groups, he did it randomly, which was better.'

'She just treated me normally whilst everyone else treated me with kid gloves. She even gave me a detention. I was kind of proud. Normal kids get detention...'

'If something tough was coming up, my psychology teacher scratched her ear to warn me. If I wasn't feeling up to it I left for a few minutes and no one said a word.'

'It only got a B, but my teacher read out my work and praised it. Then I was proud of my B.'

The take-home message is to try and treat recovering students as normally as possible and to put a positive emphasis on their achievements even if they are not at the level a student would have striven to have achieved in the past.

Specific strategies for working with students who self-harm

When supporting students suffering from or in recovery from self-harm, there are three areas schools and colleges most often ask for support with:

- whether wounds and scars should be covered

- how to minimize the harm caused by self-injury when a child is not ready to stop

- how to respond to self-harm fads and group self-harm.

I've outlined suggestions to support you with each of these areas below, though you need always to bear in mind that each individual and each school is different and different methods of support will prove successful for different students and different schools. If at all possible, it is always best to work closely with the student to decide what methods of support are proving most helpful and adapt what you are doing accordingly. Revisit your support strategies with the student regularly as the type and amount of support they require can often change quite quickly.

Should self-harm injuries and scars be covered?

There are different scenarios which might underpin our decision about whether a student's injuries and scars should be covered at school. For some students, group identity relies on self-harm — that is, those students who actively self-harm together (this is sometimes associated with Goth or Emo communities, or Justin Bieber fans). For these students, self-harm injuries may be worn almost as a badge of honour and there can be a degree of competition over the severity of the injury. This can also be the case if you have a self-harm fad doing the rounds at school (e.g. ice and salt, aerosol burns or 'chicken scratching', that is, repeatedly scratching the skin until it bleeds). Students may compete to see who has the biggest or deepest injury. In these instances, having injuries on show is very likely to trigger further incidences of self-harming behaviour and I would almost always advocate covering injuries.

Whilst some of the students who participate in this type of behaviour may be using self-harm as an unhealthy coping mechanism, the majority are simply participating in an activity that makes them feel like they belong as part of a group and the behaviour should be actively discouraged (whilst taking care to follow up with the more vulnerable individuals who may need more specific support).

I would advocate a rather different approach to those students for whom self-harm is a genuine coping mechanism and who are dealing with emotional and psychological distress.

THE RISKS OF EXPOSING INJURIES AND SCARS

In a school environment, there are some good arguments for covering self-harm injuries and scars. The most often used one is that it may be distressing for other people, and this may be true. There is often a conflict between the needs of the individual and the needs of the wider student and staff body. Educating staff and students about self-harm can help to demystify it and begin to address the stigma and fear that often surrounds it. However, one might argue that encouraging students to actively wear their wounds may normalize, and if handled inappropriately glamorize, self-harming behaviour which could have negative consequences and lead to a rise in copycat incidences.

Another argument against allowing a student to keep their injuries on show is that the attention they may receive as a result could act as a positive reinforcer for the self-harming behaviour, making it harder for them to break the self-harm cycle. They may also begin to actively identify with the label of 'self-harmer' or 'cutter' and find it hard to identify themselves another way if having their injuries on show means that this is the behaviour people most often associate them with. This can make it hard to move on, especially if their self-esteem is very low and they do not have other facets of their personality which they feel they can promote.

Finally, students may find themselves isolated, bullied or constantly questioned if their wounds are not covered. Unless they are taught how to support a friend who is self-harming, many students (and older people) do not know how best to support and may have all sorts of false beliefs about self-harm which play out in their actions. Being bullied or ignored by peers will exacerbate the low self-esteem of the student concerned and is likely to act as a maintaining factor for their self-harm.

THE RISKS OF NOT EXPOSING INJURIES AND SCARS

By this point you may feel that I strongly advocate the covering of wounds, and I certainly think that in a school environment there are some good reasons to consider this approach. However, I also think there are some compelling arguments for enabling a student to expose their injuries whilst at school.

Self-harming is not a behaviour that a student should ever be made to feel ashamed of. It is a coping mechanism and, for many students, each scar or injury has a specific meaning or trigger. To insist on covering these can further fuel the low self-esteem of the individual and make them feel ashamed or embarrassed about their behaviour. It can make them feel less willing or able to seek support when they need it as they may feel that their behaviour is being punished. This may encourage them to undertake more secretive forms of self-harm such as harming hidden parts of the body or taking non-lethal overdoses. More secretive behaviours are harder to track and respond to which may prevent the student getting the help they need when they need it.

Students who self-harm will often be left with multiple scars that they will need to live with for the rest of their life. These scars can have a huge emotional impact and learning to live with them is an important part of the recovery process. Insisting that such scars should be covered can delay recovery and can result in students developing anxious or obsessional behaviours surrounding their scars as time goes on. Enabling a student to begin to feel safe and more confident about exposing their scars within the school environment can help them to find a route forwards within wider society whilst they still have the back-up of supportive staff who know them and care for them at school.

A COMPROMISE MAY BE THE BEST ANSWER

There is no one size fits all solution: each individual case needs to be taken on its own merits bearing in mind what we know about the individual, their peers and the type and extent of injury. However, the closest I think I would be happy to come to a universal solution is to suggest that newer injuries which are still in the process of healing should be covered, both to reduce the impact of exposing such injuries on the individual and others and to promote healing, whilst wounds which are older or have formed scars should not be kept hidden unless the individual chooses to do so. In this case, I would look to work with the individual to help them feel more confident in exposing their scars if this felt like a realistic goal – in much the same way we might work to enable a student who had been scarred as a result of an accident to come to terms with their changed appearance.

How to minimize the harm caused by self-injury when a child is not ready to stop

It can be very difficult to accept that the best way to support a student to overcome their self-harming behaviours is not usually to ask them to stop immediately. Removing the coping mechanism that self-harm offers before a student has learned to use healthier coping mechanisms can put the student at great risk and has been known to lead to suicide.

If we are to accept that a student may continue to self-harm during their recovery, our next question is often 'Is there a way they might do so more safely?' This is a very sensitive topic and one that is best addressed either via the student's parents or with full parental permission if the parents do not feel comfortable having these conversations. Otherwise, there is the potential for parents to think that you are actively condoning or encouraging their child's self-harming behaviour which can lead to a breakdown of your relationship with the parents.

Harm-minimization strategies fall into three categories:

- preventing self-harm by providing thinking time or alternatives

- adapting self-harming behaviours to make them less dangerous

- wound management and infection prevention.

I've provided more information about each below.

PREVENTING SELF-HARM BY PROVIDING THINKING TIME OR ALTERNATIVES

Self-harming tends to be a very impulsive act. If we can encourage students to delay the moment of self-harming by as little as a minute, this will sometimes give them enough time to think of an alternative coping mechanism they could draw on, or provide them with the space they need to talk themselves out of self-harming. Delaying tactics tend to become increasingly helpful as recovery progresses and students develop a range of coping strategies.

Quite how the moment of self-harm is delayed depends on what the student finds most helpful. Lots of young people I've worked with have found that hiding the implement they self-harm alongside things which make them think of people or things that they love can be very helpful, for example, a picture of a parent, sibling or pet, or a letter from a friend. Keeping something of sentimental value like this with their self-harming implement can help to remind a student who is about to self-harm about the reasons not to do it and the people who care about them.

> 'I was so proud that I hadn't self-harmed for two weeks. My teacher helped me write a letter to my future self, explaining all the reasons I shouldn't self-harm and how not self-harming made me feel so proud and happy. I keep that letter with my blades and if I ever feel the urge to self-harm I make myself read the letter first. It doesn't always work, but it often does.'

Other strategies that have worked for students in recovery include keeping self-harming implements in a locked box, or in a shoebox tied up with ribbons and tape so that the implements are harder to access, or setting a phone timer or egg timer for 60 seconds and trying to wait until the time is up before asking themselves 'Do I still need to self-harm?' As recovery progresses, students will find that increasingly, a short delay can help them to overcome the urge to harm themselves.

ADAPTING SELF-HARMING BEHAVIOURS TO MAKE THEM LESS DANGEROUS

For students who cut, the likelihood of causing accidental death or losing the use of a limb can be decreased if they cut lengthwise rather than across their arms or legs. As long as students take care to avoid cutting a vein, cutting lengthwise means that there is less chance of severing a vein, artery or tendon. Similarly, cutting fleshy parts of the body such as the tops of the thighs or the stomach can decrease the risk of such injuries. However, these are areas which tend to be hidden from view, so care needs to be taken, because if a student changes from cutting their arms to cutting their thighs, you may move from a situation where you have a general idea about the extent and cleanliness of their injuries to a situation where you do not.

> I would never advocate discussing these specific harm-minimization strategies with a student without the full and informed consent of a parent. It is often better to share this information via the parents.

All students who self-harm should be taught to recognize the signs of shock, a condition caused by loss of blood, as this is relatively common following a self-harm incident. If they suspect that they may be going into shock, ideally they should seek support and tell someone what has happened, but if they feel unable to talk about their self-harming they should, as a minimum, try to get to somewhere where they will be surrounded by other people. This way, if they pass out or their health otherwise deteriorates, somebody will be able to raise the alarm. Simply heading to a populated common room or playground is fine.

SIGNS OF SHOCK

- Feeling very weak or shaky.

- Being overcome with dizziness or light-headedness.

- Feeling cold and clammy.

- Having very fast, shallow breathing.

- Being overcome with feelings of confusion or anxiety.

WOUND MANAGEMENT AND INFECTION PREVENTION

Regular self-harmers need to be taught how to manage their wounds safely in order to prevent the risk of infection. Many of the more severe outcomes that we see from self-harm injuries are as a result of infection rather than directly due to the initial wound itself.

Many students will always self-harm with the same implement and not think to clean this implement between sessions. This is a leading cause of infection but can easily be avoided by boiling the implement, soaking it in sterilizing fluids or rubbing it clean with alcohol.

It is also important that students are discouraged from sharing implements, as this is another way to spread infection. The sharing of implements frequently occurs when students are self-harming together as a part of their group identity.

Responding to self-harm fads and group self-harm

Increasingly I'm asked how schools should respond to the type of self-harm that happens in groups or the self-harm fads that work their way around schools. Group self-harm is often centred around a particular group membership, for instance, Goth or Emo groups are more likely to self-harm as a group. Other examples include Justin Bieber fans self-harming in response to the 'cuts for Bieber' craze that started online in 2013.

Group self-harm tends to be relatively superficial and without the psychological and emotional underpinnings of the self-harming behaviours discussed for the majority of this book. When self-harming as part of a group, students may proudly display their injuries as a badge of honour rather than taking steps to cover them. This is true also of self-harm fads that pass through the school which often include 'chicken scratching' and causing friction burns with erasers or aerosols. At this level, self-harm becomes a behaviour management issue rather than something deeper. However, amongst the students who self-harm very superficially, there may be one or two who go on to self-harm more seriously and secretively later on, having been triggered by this initial experience of self-harm. This is important to bear in mind.

In order to try and prevent the spread of a self-harm fad as early on as possible it can be helpful to introduce clear guidelines such as:

- injuries must be covered (this may mean long sleeves in sport/ physical education)

- self-harm on school premises is punishable in accordance with the school's behaviour policy (*not* for individual self-harmers)

- self-harm injuries and incidents should be responded to dispassionately, practically and consistently.

It is often the case that students who are participating in self-harm fads such as 'chicken scratching' do not have an understanding of the potential they have to cause themselves harm. Nor do they tend to appreciate that these behaviours may trigger a self-harm dependence in more vulnerable classmates. Often, making time in the curriculum to educate students about self-harm can be one of the best protective factors against self-harm fads starting and spreading.

Students can sensitively be taught about self-harm and how it is used as a coping mechanism for some people. It should be made clear to students exactly who they can talk to if they have concerns about themselves or a friend and an exploration of healthier coping mechanisms can be incredibly useful for all students to turn to at times of stress.

Students who are self-harming in a discrete group, where you think that the underlying reason is about group membership and group identity (rather than that several existing self-harmers have come together), may be treated similarly. There is some dispute about the best way to address such groups as some people believe that addressing the group as a whole may reinforce their feeling of group identity. This needs to be considered on a case-by-case basis. I have seen great success where proactive efforts have been taken to challenge and re-channel group identity. Some schools have supported students in setting up bands, running an event, putting on drama performances or learning a new skill, such as circus skills. It will depend on the specific students in question, but essentially the key aim is to help them find a new way of identifying themselves as a group and enabling them to communicate in more positive ways.

It is always important to talk privately with each individual, as a minority may develop a deeper psychological dependence on self-harm. Individuals should also be followed up some months later as any student who has self-harmed once is more likely than their peers to turn to secretly self-harming in the future as a means of coping with a difficult situation or feelings they cannot control.

On rare occasions, a whole group can become very dependent on self-harm and find it hard to stop in the same way that an individual might. In this case you will need to go further than simply treating their self-harm as a behavioural issue. It can help to have a teacher or counsellor work with the individual members on activities that build on self-esteem and communication, or with the group as a whole, so long as discussion of self-harm itself was not the focus of the activities.

Sometimes, several students who self-harm come together to form a group – this may be either to support each other in continuing to self-harm or supporting each other in recovery. Either way, this kind of friendship group has the potential either to provide very good support, or to do great harm to the individuals involved, and needs careful management and guidance. It is best to try and gain a full and thorough understanding of the relationships within the group and the positives and negatives for each individual before deciding how best to proceed.

You will find this process is most informative if you talk to each student individually.

GROUND RULES FOR GROUPS

Working with the group to form ground rules can help to keep each group member safe. You should not impose these ground rules, but rather come to them as a result of group discussion. The kinds of ground rules that might be appropriate for the group to agree include:

- We will work together to promote recovery, not self-harm.

- We will not share ideas for lying about or hiding our self-harm.

- We will share ideas that are working for us in overcoming the urge to self-harm.

- It's okay for us to tell a trusted adult if we're worried about ourselves or a friend.

- We will not self-harm together (you may need to work towards this).

- We will not discuss the specifics of self-harming, as this can be upsetting or triggering, but we will share more general feelings.

- If our friend is finding it too hard to listen to us talk about our feelings, it is okay for them to ask us to talk to a trusted adult instead.

- We will celebrate each other's recovery successes.

- We will never judge each other based on the severity or frequency of our self-harm.

- We will trust and respect each other.

- If somebody wants to leave the group, we will respect that and welcome them back any time they feel they need our support.

Benefits of students being friends with other students who self-harm

- They feel less alone.

- They have people to talk to who understand them.

- They can provide each other with support during recovery.

- They can help to keep each other safe.

- They can share recovery strategies.

Dangers of students being friends with other students who self-harm

- Self-harming is normalized and motivation to overcome it decreases.

- They are able to share self-harming techniques.

- They can share tips for hiding or lying about self-harm.

- They can feel they have to self-harm or they'll lose their friends.

- Being friends with people who self-harm is stressful and may increase each individual's vulnerability.

- New and more dangerous self-harm techniques are more likely to be explored as a group, or by an individual encouraged by a group.

The best approach will vary depending on the individuals involved and the group dynamics. But a generally helpful approach is to work with the group on building self-esteem, communication skills and problem-solving skills and to work with each individual on specific aspects of their self-harming and recovery plan.

Specific strategies for working with students suffering from eating disorders

When supporting students suffering from or in recovery from eating disorders, there are three areas schools and colleges most often ask for support with:

- supervising mealtimes

- participation in school sports

- what not to say.

I've outlined suggestions to support you with each of these areas below, though you need always to bear in mind that each individual is different and different methods of support will prove successful for different students. If at all possible, it is always best to work closely with the student to decide what methods of support are proving most helpful and adapt what you are doing accordingly. Revisit your support strategies with the student regularly as the type and amount of support they require can often change quite quickly.

Ideas to help at mealtimes

School staff working with students suffering or recovering from an eating disorder often find themselves in a situation where they want to offer support at mealtimes, but they don't know how best to help. It will depend entirely on the individual and, as long as they are well enough, you should always be guided by the student in question, but here are some tried and tested suggestions you might like to implement.

THINK ABOUT MEAL TIMINGS AND LOCATIONS

The school lunch hall or cafeteria can be a difficult place for someone recovering from an eating disorder to spend time in. You should never insist that their meals are taken there, even if it is your school's usual policy. Perhaps your school has more than one lunch sitting and the student would feel okay in the cafeteria at a time when their peers aren't there, or perhaps you should find somewhere different altogether, such as a classroom.

TRUST THEM TO KEEP THEIR OWN FOOD DIARY

Many students recovering from an eating disorder are expected to keep a food diary. It can be very tempting to complete this on their behalf because you know what they have eaten and are keen to ensure that it is recorded accurately. However, it can be an important show of trust to allow the student to complete their own food diary. Of course, if you have reason to suspect it is wildly inaccurate then you'll need to rethink this approach.

LET THEM EAT WITH A FRIEND OR PARENT

Having a friend or a trusted adult with them whilst they eat can make a lot of students feel more at ease. If you arrange for this, you should ask specifically whether the friend should also be eating at the same time. Some students will not feel comfortable eating whilst their friend is not, whilst others will want to focus on their meal but would like their friend just to talk to them, usually about something entirely non-food related if possible.

In some instances it may be appropriate to invite a student's parent in to school to support them through lunch. Treatment often involves training a parent to support their child through mealtimes, so facilitating the continuation of this support until the student is feeling more stable and more ready to eat independent of a parent can be a helpful step in the recovery process.

PROVIDE SPECIFIC MEALS

If it's practical, you can agree meals ahead with the student and their parents and have the school provide them (or they may bring their own packed lunch). This will enable them to stick with foods they feel safe with and will also add some predictability to their meals which can help them feel safe. Equally, you may find that if 'normal' school meals must be taken, making the student aware of what meal will be provided beforehand will help them to prepare themselves (though for others it will give them longer to worry, so you need to decide what is right for each individual).

LET THEM SERVE THEMSELVES

Even if it is not the done thing in your school canteen, it may be helpful to allow the student to serve their own food. For some students, this helps them to feel more in control of the meal and learning to serve and consume reasonable portions of food is an important skill for the student to master. However, some students find it easier to treat food like medicine in the early days and will eat the prescribed amount they are provided with, but feel far more guilty about eating food which they have put on their plate of their own volition, so you need to discuss the best approach on a case-by-case basis, and to bear in mind that the best strategy for a student may change as their recovery progresses.

DON'T 'WATCH'

Make sure that, even if you are supervising a meal, the student never feels like they're being overtly watched or spied upon as this will make them feel deeply uncomfortable (it would make just about anyone feel deeply uncomfortable!). If it's necessary for you to supervise a meal then having a prop such as some marking or a book or similar to make it clear that you're not staring constantly at the student can help to make them feel a little more at ease.

DON'T TALK ABOUT HOW MUCH THEY'VE EATEN

This can be really hard, especially if they've done really well and you want to congratulate them, but it's generally not a good idea to pass comment. 'Well done for eating half a jacket potato, that's fantastic!' can so easily be heard as 'Oh my God, I can't believe you ate so much, you're so greedy.' If they volunteer that they are pleased with what they've eaten, a safe reply is something along the lines of 'Well done, I realize that must have been really difficult for you.'

DON'T DISCUSS FOOD AND WEIGHT CONCERNS OVER LUNCH

If possible, steer the conversation as far away as possible from concerns about food and weight. If the student instigates a conversation about difficult feelings, or their weight or food, then acknowledge that it's an important conversation but not one you feel you should be having right now. Suggest a more appropriate time to return to it later.

AFTER LUNCH MATTERS TOO

After they've eaten, students recovering from eating disorders will often feel really panicky, depressed, guilty or ashamed and some may try and purge themselves of the calories they've consumed, for example, by vomiting, using laxatives or exercising. At this moment, they are also at high risk of self-harm. For these reasons it's really helpful to make sure that the student is kept busy for half an hour after they've finished lunch and not left alone with their feelings.

Safe participation in school sports

The sports department need to be involved in the recovery of any student with an eating disorder whether they are overweight, underweight or within an acceptable weight range. Below I've focused on working with students who are recovering from anorexia as this is an area that school staff often feel most unsure about.

OVER-EXERCISE AND ANOREXIA NERVOSA

If left unmonitored students suffering from anorexia nervosa will often choose to exercise hard for many hours a day in order to burn calories. This level of activity is clearly unacceptable during recovery, but removing the ability to exercise or participate in sport at all can be detrimental to their long-term recovery. It is important that students who habitually over-exercise learn to form a more healthy relationship with exercise in the same way that they must improve their relationship with food.

THE SOCIAL ASPECT OF SCHOOL SPORT

There is a certain extent to which it is important to try and include a student recovering from an eating disorder in as many normal school activities as possible – and sport/physical education is no exception. Exempting a student from sport quickly marks them out as different from their peers, which can feel stressful for them and lead to questioning and sometimes teasing.

SEEK GUIDANCE FROM HEALTH PROVIDERS

If the student is in some form of treatment, it is a good idea to approach their health providers to discuss what would be an appropriate level of sporting activity for them to be participating in. At its most extreme, anorexia can result in patients being prescribed complete bed rest whilst their bodies are re-nourished. However, if a student is considered well enough to attend school, then it is likely that their health practitioner will condone some level of exercise.

WORK WITH THE STUDENT TO AGREE A HEALTHY EXERCISE PLAN

As ever, it is important to ensure that the student is allowed to feel some sense of control over their own life. Rather than being told exactly how much exercise they can do, and when, this should form the basis of a discussion between the student, the school, their health practitioners and their parents. If the student desperately wants to be involved in a sporting activity at a level or intensity that is considered inappropriate by their health provider then, instead of telling the student 'no', work together to decide what other recovery targets must be met before they are able to participate. Also, try to think of ways to work towards these targets and to gradually increase their participation in their chosen sport.

WORK WITH PARENTS

Where possible, parents should be involved throughout the conversation, but if this is not the case you should inform parents about the exercise plan agreed for their child. It's important that they are aware of how much and what types of exercise it is appropriate for their child to be taking as they will be responsible for monitoring the student's exercise habits outside of school hours. Make sure that the lines of communication are open or you may find a situation where the student plays the school off against their parents, allowing each to believe they are doing no exercise in the other setting.

EXERCISE DIARIES

In more extreme cases, and particularly where a student is learning to overcome a compulsion to over-exercise, an exercise diary can be a helpful tool. Where relevant, this is something that can be used to form the basis for discussion during treatment sessions so the student could choose to record thoughts and feelings in addition to details about the amount and type of exercise undertaken.

DETERMINE WHICH TYPES OF ACTIVITIES ARE MOST ACCEPTABLE

As well as the amount of exercise to be taken, there should be some discussion around the type of exercise that is appropriate. If, for example, a student has been obsessively using gym equipment or cross country running in a quest to lose weight, this form of exercise may have extremely unhealthy associations for them and they may struggle to undertake this activity in a measured way. It can often make sense to avoid 'trigger sports' during the early days of recovery. Equally, it may be inappropriate to allow a student to participate in a sport to competition level as their perfectionism and drive to succeed can make it difficult for them to avoid over-exercising and they may not be psychologically ready to be put into a highly competitive situation.

Additionally, sports which have weight category requirements are likely to be inappropriate until the student is at an advanced stage of recovery. Again, their healthcare practitioner will be able to offer sound guidance on these points.

ENSURE WEIGHT/PHYSIQUE IS NOT A FOCAL POINT FOR COACHES

Any sports coach or physical education teacher working with the student, either within school hours or extracurricularly, should be made aware of their eating disorder (with the student's permission) so that they can help the student to exercise in a healthy way. It is paramount that they do not make comments about the student's physical appearance or weight, even if they perceive their comments to be positive.

EXERCISE AND SPORT AS A MEANS OF RELIEVING STRESS

If an appropriate balance is found, sport and exercise can be a very positive outlet for a student's stress during the difficult process of recovery. Lower-impact options which also have a wellbeing focus, like yoga or Pilates, are well worth considering.

Students in recovery – what not to say

A great degree of sensitivity is needed when interacting with a student recovering from any form of eating disorder. Their self-esteem is very low and they are in a very vulnerable position where they will believe and blow out of all proportion even the slightest negative comment (or even positive comments which they may reinterpret as negative). Here are some key flashpoints to avoid.

AVOID COMMENTING ON THE STUDENT'S APPEARANCE

During the recovery process, it can be very easy for eating-disordered thoughts to be triggered by someone saying or doing the wrong thing, even if they mean well. Almost any comment on appearance can be reinterpreted by the student as 'You're fat.'

Well-meaning comments such as 'You're looking healthy', 'It's great to see some colour in your cheeks' or 'You must feel better now you have more energy' are all open to misinterpretation. It's best to avoid any comment at all on a student's appearance.

CONSIDER LESSON CONTENT

It's also important to be sensitive to tasks in class that may be difficult for the recovering student and to consider altering your scheme of work as necessary. Any tasks involving food, healthy eating and exercise, weighing or measuring the body in any way, or discussion of eating disorders are best avoided. If this is not possible, show the student all of the materials beforehand and allow them to opt out if they prefer.

DON'T DEFINE THE STUDENT BY THEIR EATING DISORDER

Especially if a student has been very ill, it can be difficult to remember almost anything about them other than the eating disorder which has consumed them for so long. You must try and avoid this though. The student will not want to be constantly bombarded with questions about their eating disorder or even have to put up with continuous oblique references to it. Instead make an effort to remember the student's strengths and interests before their eating disorder took over and drive conversation here wherever possible.

Preparing for holidays

The school calendar is punctuated by frequent holidays and these can be a cause of real stress for students who are struggling with their mental health or emotional wellbeing. For these students, school often provides the routine and motivation to get up that they need to keep depression at bay, and the support they need to keep their emotional wellbeing in check. So it's important that you prepare students you're working with for periods when they cannot access help at school. The advice that follows is designed for use in the run-up to school holidays; however, for your most vulnerable students, you may want to consider how you could adapt this to prepare students for weekends too.

Discuss how they're feeling about the holidays

Discuss with the student how they're feeling about the upcoming holidays and whether there is anything specific that is giving them cause for concern. In addition to the fact that they may not have access to their usual support network and the structure and stability of school, they may have specific concerns about:

- travelling

- spending time with specific people or in specific places

- responsibilities at home

- schoolwork for completion over the holidays.

Have an open discussion with them and generate a list of issues they are concerned about and be sure that you address each of these in turn. Try to gain an understanding of why each item on the list is causing the student anxiety as well as thinking of possible ways around it. Try to encourage the student to think up their own solutions where possible, rather than just feeding them the answers as this will better prepare them for facing any unexpected difficulties they may face over the holiday period.

Discuss who is currently aware of their difficulties
Talk with the student about who, beyond school, is currently aware of what they're going through and what support they've been receiving. Depending on who knows what, it might be appropriate to discuss with the student how you might work with them to increase the number of people who have enough information to be able to provide effective support.

Consider who they can turn to for help at home
Who knows and who can help are sometimes two different things. Out of the people who are aware of what's going on with the student, discuss who they might turn to if things become difficult or they need someone to talk to.

Think about what other sources of support are available
Identify further sources of support with the student. This is likely to include helplines and websites. Try to identify at least one source of support that is available 24/7.

Think about what their typical day will look like – how will they ensure structure and routine?
Think with the student about how they are going to spend their time over the holiday. The structure and routine of school can help to stave off depression and anxiety which often lay almost dormant until the

holidays arrive, bringing with them a lack of structure and no reason to get up, get dressed or get out. Think about simple aims that you might agree with the student, such as 'I will leave the house for at least 20 minutes each day. If I have no other reason, I will walk to the local shop and back again.'

Think about how they might add routine to an otherwise unstructured day. This might include taking on household chores like emptying the dishwasher, preparing meals, walking the dog or watering the garden. Alternatively they might agree a schedule to regularly meet friends or choose to take up a holiday job or voluntary position which provides them with motivation and structure.

Explore the healthy coping mechanisms they can turn to

Finally, consider with the student what healthy coping mechanisms they might use if they aren't managing. Rather than turning to unhealthy coping like self-harm, bingeing or abusing alcohol, think with them about how they might work through their feelings in another way, such as by painting, writing or playing sport.

How to support a student who is having a panic attack

The final part of this chapter is dedicated to teaching you how you can best support a student who is suffering from a panic attack. Students suffering from self-harm or eating disorders may experience anxiety, panic and panic attacks and sometimes the frequency and intensity of these may increase temporarily as they try to reduce their reliance on unhealthy coping behaviours. Responding appropriately can minimize the length and severity of an attack. You can also work with a student to help try to prevent future attacks. I've provided guidance below, but you should discuss all of these ideas with the individual as what may quell panic in some people may trigger it in someone else.

Just be there

Having a panic attack is a terrifying feeling and one that can make you feel very alone. Just being present can make a huge difference to the person who is suffering. It will make them feel a little less out of control of the situation, which is likely to shorten the duration of the attack. Unless it's absolutely necessary, don't leave the student alone whilst they're having a panic attack. Call for help or send someone else, but remain steadfast by the student's side and remind them that you are there and that you will not leave them.

Assert control

There are several feelings that accompany a panic attack, but one universal feeling is a loss of control, both of the general situation and of the sufferer's own body. When your heart is racing, your breathing is out of control and you feel like you might die, it's hard to feel in control of things. Try to gently assert control of the situation as this can feel deeply reassuring for the sufferer. You might not feel very in control but it's time to employ your best acting skills. Talk in a calm, measured manner, explain simply and carefully what is happening now, what you are doing to help and what will happen next. It almost doesn't matter what you say so long as you say it with some authority and you are apparently in control of the situation.

Don't panic

Panic fuels panic so it's most important that you control your own anxiety when responding to someone else's panic attack. If necessary, you may also need to take active steps to calm down others too. It's possible for one panic attack to trigger a kind of mass hysteria as people set each other off. This is a moment to really assert your control and appear authoritative. Be polite but firm in telling other people to move away from the sufferer, to give them some space. Encourage people not to crowd, run, scream or otherwise panic.

Don't make assumptions or be dismissive

Don't assume that you know what has caused the panic attack, don't assume to understand and don't be dismissive of the cause if it becomes clear. This is not a time for platitudes... Panic attacks can often be an extreme reaction to a relatively minor trigger but that does not make them feel any less terrifying to the sufferer who will often feel like they are dying. Being told not to be silly, or that there's nothing to worry about is insensitive at best and panic-fuelling at worst.

Move away from the cause

If the cause of the attack becomes clear, move away from it, or have it removed. It may be irrational and you may not understand why this trigger is fuelling such panic, but that is irrelevant right now. What is important is to put some distance between the sufferer and the trigger so that they can begin to gain some control.

Focus on breathing

It can really help a panic attack to pass if the sufferer is able to take control of their breathing. Some people advocate the use of breathing into a paper bag, others try to slow the sufferer's breathing by counting with them as they breathe in and out, and another strategy is to imagine blowing bubbles. It doesn't really matter what strategy you use, but sit with the sufferer, talk to them about their breathing, encourage them to actively think about it and really focus on slowing it down and taking control of it. This may take some time and you may have to repeat yourself frequently. Stick with it. You will get there. Taking quite a physical approach can help too. Holding the sufferer by the shoulders and talking to them face on can help some people; others like to have their hand held whilst you talk to them from their side. You will soon get a feel for what is working.

Give the sufferer space and time

Once the immediate signs of the panic attack have passed, many people assume that the sufferer should be able to continue as normal, but this is not the case. It can take quite some time to 'come down' from a panic attack and if possible the sufferer should be given space and time to recover before being expected to continue with, for example, lessons at school. During this time it's helpful if they can be accompanied and be somewhere where they feel safe without feeling they have to talk about anything unless they want to. Some people find walking is helpful whilst others like to watch TV or listen to music to help take their mind off whatever it was that triggered the attack.

Afterwards, identify the trigger

A few hours later, or the next day, when the sufferer is fully recovered and ready to talk about things, it is worth gently exploring what triggered the attack and thinking about ways that this trigger might be avoided in future. It is also worth discussing what was helpful to them in terms of supporting them to overcome the attack; this will enable you to provide better support on future occasions. It is worth ensuring that school staff, friends and family are made aware of anything specific the student finds helpful when trying to overcome an attack.

Don't be afraid to talk about it

Panic attacks are horrible experiences and sufferers often feel embarrassed or ashamed by them. Ensure that the student does not feel stigmatized by their attacks by being willing to talk about it with them and trying to understand more about how they feel and how you can help. The more we talk about these things the more we understand and the better we are able to help. Additionally, the more open a sufferer is able to be about their panic attacks, the more likely they are to be able to feel confident telling someone when they feel the early signs of an attack coming on which can be a good way of preventing attacks from escalating in the first instance.

LEARNING TO TAKE AWAY FROM THIS CHAPTER

- There are a range of ways you can support students in recovery. Different students will find different approaches helpful so it's important to work with the individual rather than make assumptions based on past experience.

- Regular access to a trusted adult can provide stability and support to students who may use this opportunity to discuss how to overcome practical difficulties they're facing day to day at school.

- The holidays can be a difficult time for students in recovery from self-harm and eating disorders. It's important to work with them to prepare for the holidays when they will not be able to draw on the support, guidance and stability usually available for them at school.

THINGS TO DO

- Think about how to implement simple strategies to support students in recovery such as the use of free passes, a bolt hole or providing regular access to a trusted adult.

- Create a simple form you can work through with vulnerable students to prepare them for any upcoming holiday periods using the ideas shared in this chapter.

- Make staff aware of the best way to support students who are having a panic attack and discuss these guidelines with any student who experiences panic attacks to see how they can be best adapted to meet the needs of that individual.

CHAPTER 13

The Impact of the Internet

This chapter will enable you to:

- understand the support that some students find in online friends and networks

- define slang terms commonly used by people discussing self-harm and eating disorders online

- understand what pro-ana, pro-mia and pro-harm sites are and why they are dangerous

- implement practical strategies to prevent students from accessing harmful sites

- safely, rather than suddenly, support a student to stop accessing harmful 'pro' sites and networks.

Increasingly, people of all ages turn to the internet as a form of support for all manner of different issues – you may have looked online for advice about how to help the students in your care with their difficulties with self-harm or eating disorders before coming across this book. There's a lot of helpful information and support available online and it's important that we remember that the internet can be a tool for support as well as having a potential role in fuelling and exacerbating some students' difficulties.

At a time when a student may find themselves increasingly isolated by their difficulties, online support forums and social networks can provide access to other people who are able to understand and support. A student may actively push their friends away, worried that there will be a lack of understanding or support or about the potential for bullying. Meanwhile, they may actively seek support from other students struggling with the same self-harm or eating-disordered behaviours online. This was the case for 16-year-old Sam and 12-year-old Amy-Lea:

Case study: Sam, 16, anorexia nervosa

As my illness took over, I talked to less and less people in real life. I felt like they didn't understand me any more and that all they ever did was try and change me, or tell me what to do. They never cared about what I wanted or how I felt. For quite a few weeks I spent a lot of time all by myself, not talking to anyone at school or at home, just hiding. After a while, I came across an online forum where I was able to talk to other people like me. I felt like they really 'got me'. They didn't judge or criticize me, they didn't try to change me. It was the first time I felt listened to and supported in a long time and it gave me a lot of strength.

Case study: Amy-Lea, 12, self-harming

I couldn't talk to anyone about my burns. I was sort of ashamed and embarrassed all at the same time. All those mixed-up feelings kind of meant I couldn't find a way to tell my friends or my teachers or my parents…but the thing was that it was kind of a really big part of my life at that time and I felt like I needed to talk to someone. After a while, I made some friends online who were facing similar problems and who were cutting or burning like me. It made me feel less alone, knowing there were other people who were behaving the same way and who understood how I felt and what I was doing. Also, it was really good because I found it hard to sleep a lot of the time, but because I had friends all over the world online, there was always someone I could talk to, even in the middle of the night. Being able to talk to my friends online at night helped me to panic less and probably stopped me burning as much as I would have done otherwise because I tended to do it most when I was upset or panicking, especially at night time when I felt really on my own.

As Sam and Amy-Lea's experiences show, online support can be very helpful for a student who might be feeling otherwise alone and unsure where to turn. However, the online world is not always a safe place for vulnerable students and there are specific sites which aim to promote unhealthy behaviours such as restricting food intake, purging, self-harming or over-exercising.

LIST OF EATING DISORDERS AND SELF-HARM SLANG TERMS COMMONLY USED ONLINE

Ana: Slang term for anorexia, often talked about as if 'Ana' were a friend.

Bikini bridge: When a girl in a bikini lies down and her hip bones protrude well past their stomach causing their bikini bottom to stretch across, so a gap is formed. This is as a result of low weight.

Criss-cross: Self-harm injuries (sometimes in a criss-cross pattern).

Cutter: Someone who self-harms by cutting themselves.

Ed: Slang term for eating disorders, often talked about as if 'Ed' were a friend.

Fitspiration: Images, videos and quotes designed to inspire exercise/body building.

Fitspo: Slang term for fitspiration.

Food porn: Pictures of food, often beautifully presented. In many cases sufferers share pictures instead of eating and the pictures may represent a food they are craving or are especially proud of avoiding.

Goal weight: In treatment this would denote a healthy weight a sufferer is aiming for; online it is more likely to refer to a low weight that a sufferer is trying to achieve.

Mia: Slang term for bulimia, often talked about as if 'Mia' were a friend.

Pro-ana site: Website that promotes anorexia.

Pro-harm site: Website that promotes self-harm (also referred to as pro-injury, pro-self-injury, pro-self-harm or pro-cutting).

Pro-mia site: Website that promotes bulimia.

Reverse thinspo: Images of, for example, overweight people designed to discourage sufferers from eating for fear of what may happen to them if they do (i.e. they too may become overweight).

Ripped: Muscly – often used by boys who are over-exercising.

Slashing: Self-harming by cutting oneself.

Thigh gap: A space between the inner thighs when standing upright with both knees touching as a result of low weight.

Thinspo: Slang term for thinspiration.

Thinspiration: Images, videos and quotes to inspire weight loss.

Trigger: Something that exacerbates self-harming or eating-disordered behaviours.

Wannerexic: Someone who does not meet the diagnostic criteria of anorexia but who yearns to develop the illness as a means of dieting. Often used as a derogatory term by anorexics.

Pro-ana, pro-mia and pro-harm sites

Pro-ana, pro-mia and pro-harm sites are websites that promote anorexic, bulimic and self-harming lifestyles. They do not tend to set out to promote eating-disordered or self-harming behaviours to those who have not already developed them, and the sites often have disclaimers warning those who have not already developed such difficulties not to enter. The sites consider eating disorders and self-harming as lifestyle choices rather than illnesses or issues to overcome. The sites are often set up by people who are suffering with self-harming or eating-disordered behaviours themselves and who are looking to validate their illness and seek support to continue with their behaviours from fellow sufferers.

These sites vary hugely in their precise content though they share the goal of supporting sufferers to continue their harmful behaviours. Pro-ana and pro-mia sites are often a forum for people to exchange pictures and weight loss or purging tips and to encourage one another's weight loss whilst pro-harm sites often explore different ways of harming and ways for hiding behaviours and injuries so that self-harm can remain undetected.

In addition to specific sites, pro-ana, pro-mia and pro-harm material is shared widely via social media networks and especially image-sharing sites such as Instagram and Tumblr. For example, there are dozens of accounts on Instagram and Tumblr dedicated solely to sharing images of 'bikini bridges' whilst other accounts specialize in 'thigh gaps'. There are yet more accounts dedicated to sharing 'thinspo' and 'fitspo' images and quotes and many sufferers will share images via their personal social media accounts using 'thinspo' or 'fitspo' hashtags.

Who uses pro-ana, pro-mia and pro-harm sites?

These sites are often a refuge for people suffering from eating disorders and self-harm. It's common for sufferers to feel quite isolated, having pushed away their family and friends, preferring to seek out like-minded individuals online. There are over 500 such sites and the latest studies predict that they attract more than 500,000 unique visitors a year, of which the majority are teenage girls and one in five is aged between six and 11.

Why are the sites dangerous?

Pro-sites are dangerous because they encourage users to embrace unhealthy behaviours, seeing self-harming and eating-disordered behaviours as a lifestyle choice rather than difficulties to overcome. The sites share tips and tricks designed to maintain or exacerbate eating-disordered and self-harming behaviours and there is often a support network which will encourage people to consume ever fewer calories, purge longer and harder or cut more frequently or more deeply. With most things in life, if you have a good teacher and a good support network then your skills in, and dedication to, a particular topic will increase more quickly. This is true also of self-harm and eating disorders whose onset can be expedited and symptoms exacerbated by pro-ana, pro-mia and pro-harm sites. The sites also make recovery far harder, as they contradict anything a student may be told about the benefits of recovery and the downsides of eating disorders and self-harm.

Some students come across these sites inadvertently whilst looking for support to overcome their difficulties – it can be easy for them to get sucked in by the strong community and sense of belonging they feel, and also by the normalization and acceptance of unhealthy behaviours. Many students find it very hard to leave these sites and communities once they begin to feel accepted by them. The case studies of Peter and Danny below demonstrate how students can get drawn into becoming a part of a pro-community.

Case study: Danny, 14, self-harming

I tried to tell one of my friends that I'd been cutting, but she totally freaked out which kinda put me off telling anyone else. But my cutting was getting a bit out of hand so I needed to talk to someone about it, so I went online. I was looking for help about how to stop and came across this site where everyone was so helpful and nice and understanding. But they didn't think I should stop, they said it was a way for me to express myself and helped me realize that it wasn't a problem if I felt a need to cut myself. I got to know a few people really well and they became like best friends really. I talked to them about stuff I never felt I could talk to anyone about before. Sometimes we would cut at the same time and talk about how we felt and share pictures and videos of our cutting too. It always made me feel better and like I was a part of something and not alone. We would all share ideas about different ways to cut and also practical stuff about how to make sure no one found out and good excuses you could use if someone saw your cuts, things like that.

I kept talking to my friends on the site and cutting with them for quite a few months. One day a new member came who reminded me of myself. She was looking for a way to stop cutting and I found myself telling her she shouldn't and telling her all the reasons why. Then I suddenly kind of saw myself in her and wondered if it was a good thing to be encouraging her cutting and also whether it was a good thing that I'd found the site that day I needed help. Would things be different now if I had found some support to stop cutting instead of carrying on? I began to wonder if maybe the site was a bad thing after all. It was very hard to leave though, I had a lot of good friends there and they all told me not to go. It took a long time to build up the courage to leave and I only managed it once I'd finally been brave enough to tell a teacher who helped me think about how I could leave the site but still feel supported in other ways.

Case study: Peter, 15, anorexia nervosa

I got in with this group of lads online who were really into health and fitness like me. We would talk about our workouts, what we were eating and what supplements we were taking. We were really competitive and would share pictures to show how ripped we were and would share our weight and measurements, details of the exercise we'd done that day and how many calories we'd consumed. We'd always be egging each other on to do more exercise and eat less and we were always vying to be the best, to be the one who did the most push-ups or ran the fastest on the running machine for the longest time or who lifted the heaviest weights. It really spurred me on and helped me to increase how much exercise I was doing and decrease how much I was eating. I knew that if I slipped up then I'd be letting everyone down as whilst it was competitive, there was also this feeling that we were doing it together. Talking about my health and fitness online became almost as much of an obsession as actually preparing my food and doing my exercise and stuff. I'd be up half the night chatting online about the best way to burn calories or improve muscle tone. It totally took over my life. It was only when I suddenly got really ill and was rushed to hospital, where all my access to the internet was cut off at first, that I realized what a big part of my life it had become.

How we can help to prevent the use of pro-ana,
pro-mia and pro-harm sites

There are several practical approaches we can take to help prevent vulnerable students from using pro-sites:

- Highlight safe sources of information.

- Educate students about self-harm and eating disorders.

- Educate students about the potential dangers of pro-sites.

- Encourage students to share their concerns about their friends.

These approaches are outlined more fully below. Many of these ideas are about general awareness-raising and are messages that can usefully be conveyed to the entire student body rather than just those known to be at risk. This can be a beneficial approach as it will ensure that those students who are vulnerable, but not yet known to us to be vulnerable, will receive the information. Additionally, it enables and empowers peers to look out for and support each other.

Many students come across pro-sites when they are in the early stages of developing self-harming or eating-disordered behaviours and they turn to the internet whilst on the lookout for information or support. Whilst they may want to find an alternative to the unhealthy behaviours they are developing, if they come across pro-ana, pro-mia or pro-harm sites instead, they may find themselves quickly catapulted into a terrifying new world where their harmful behaviours rapidly develop even if they had not intended for that to happen.

In order to prevent students accidentally coming across pro-sites whilst looking for genuine sources of support to overcome their difficulties, it's important that we clearly signpost safe sources of support. There is some excellent, safe, support available both online and offline, but students will not necessarily know the difference between trusted and untrusted sources of support unless safe sites are specifically highlighted to them. You can do this in a variety of ways. Posters at school are a great start, and talking about sources of support to turn to during times of need within appropriate lessons can also be very helpful.

We can also decrease the likelihood of students falling into a habit of self-harming or eating-disordered behaviour after stumbling across it online if we have taken the time to educate them about self-harm and eating disorders. Students need to understand that eating disorders are serious mental health conditions and that self-harm is a coping mechanism that poses considerable health risks. None of these behaviours are 'lifestyle choices' as suggested by pro-sites. They are unhealthy coping mechanisms which sufferers may need significant support to overcome. Providing students with a better understanding about self-harm and eating disorders will empower them to make better choices when faced with these issues online and will help to protect them from becoming consumed by dangerous online subcultures. It will also help them to recognize where there are issues that need to be addressed with their peers.

We can also educate students about the potential dangers of pro-sites to ensure that they understand the possible ramifications of using such sites. Many people worry that by highlighting the fact that pro-sites exist we may encourage vulnerable students to seek them out. This may be true to a certain extent, so you always need to make a judgement call based on your knowledge of a specific group of students. However, I cannot help but feel that it is unlikely that those at risk would not come across these sites even without them being highlighted and that if we teach about them within a broader context then the protective factors will outweigh the risks.

We should actively encourage students to share their concerns about their friends. Often, friends can be the first to pick up the early warning signs of eating disorders or self-harming behaviours and they may be aware that their friend is actively using pro-ana, pro-mia or pro-harm sites (though they are likely to refer to them in quite a different way). Explain to students who they should talk to if they're concerned about a friend, why it's important and what's likely to happen next. Teach students that a good friend is one who supports and looks out for a friend when they're in need and that alerting a teacher or parent to the fact that their friend may be visiting harmful websites will benefit their friend in the long run as they will be provided with the support they need to overcome their difficulties. However, their friend might be angry in the short term.

SAFELY EDUCATING STUDENTS ABOUT PRO-SITES

In safely educating students about pro-sites about pro-ana, pro-mia and pro-harm sites we can:

- educate them more generally about eating disorders and self-harm

- signpost sources of safe support, both online and offline

- explore the risks of using 'pro' sites and material online

- highlight who they can talk to at school if they are currently using such sites

- discuss strategies for 'weaning themselves off' these sites

- consider warning signs that a friend might be using these sites

- encourage students to seek help if they are worried about a friend.

What to do if you're concerned

If you suspect that a student is using harmful sites, or a student has shared concerns about a friend, then it's vital that you intervene. Talk openly to the student and allow them to share any concerns they currently have with you. You need to listen and ask plenty of open questions and be prepared to act on what you find out.

It is unadvisable for a student's access to harmful sites to be very suddenly withdrawn as doing so without putting alternative support and coping strategies in place can be very dangerous and put a student at great risk. Whilst it is clear to us that the sites are harmful, the student using them is likely to feel a great deal of support from their online friends and may have no one else they feel they can talk to about their concerns. The case study below explores how Aisha felt when her access to the internet was suddenly and completely withdrawn.

Case study: Aisha, 18, anorexia nervosa

My mum found out I was using this pro-ana site and completely flipped out. She'd read some article about how dangerous they were and was convinced that it was almost solely to blame for my illness. She took away my laptop and my phone and made sure I had no way of accessing the internet at all. It felt like being put in prison. I had not left the house for weeks and my whole world was online. I had friends and a life there and people I could talk to about the things that worried me and stressed me out. Yes, we were all encouraging each other to eat less and exercise more and yes, I got a buzz every time I shared a picture of myself with more ribs showing and I got nice feedback, but as well as what I now see as the unhealthy side of it, there was the healthy support. People I could talk to, people who didn't judge me, who listened to me and cared about what I had to say.

When my mum stopped me going online that day, I suddenly felt so helpless. I felt like I had nothing left to live for. I took a load of sleeping pills. I wanted to go to sleep and never wake up because I had no life left.

How we can safely stop a student from using harmful pro-sites

If it becomes clear that a student is using harmful sites, then it's important that we support them to stop. The key strategies we can employ to help them are to:

- understand why they're using the sites

- explore other sources of support that meet their needs

- agree on a plan for decreasing site usage

- ensure they are receiving support to address their underlying difficulties.

It's important that we take time to talk to students about why they're using pro-ana, pro-mia or pro-harm sites. This both gives the student the message that we are not judging them and are keen to hear what they have to say, and also provides us with important information we can use to help us to wean the student off the sites. Different people have different motivations for using such sites and depending on the student's specific motivations, you may explore different alternative coping strategies.

Once you've got a general understanding of the reasons that a student has for using pro-sites, you can begin to explore alternatives with them. Some common examples include:

- If the student feels unable to communicate face to face and prefers to talk online, explore safe online support forums with them or consider whether using a mechanism such as an instant messaging tool could help them feel more comfortable talking to a trusted adult.

- If the student feels that they do not have friends in the real world, only online, think with them about who they used to be friends with before they started having difficulties and how these friendships might be revisited and redeveloped.

- If the student says that the only people who understand them are the people on the site they've been using, try to find ways to help them explore and explain their issues and feelings which might make it a little easier for a trusted adult or friend to understand.

- If the student says that they really enjoyed the positive reinforcement they got when they posted information or pictures about their harmful behaviours, think about ways you can build encouragement and praise into their recovery programme. If they respond well to praise then this could prove to be a very helpful way of encouraging healthier behaviours during their recovery.

When it comes to reducing a student's usage of harmful sites, you'll need to work with them and their parents, who may feel strongly that their child's internet use should be completely withdrawn. However, suddenly removing a student's internet access or deleting their online profiles is likely to be counter-productive. Instead taking a controlled, respectful approach is likely to be more successful. Asking the student to keep a log of when they're using the sites and why can be a helpful start. This can help you to baseline how much they are using the sites and what they are getting out of it. Work with the student towards reduced site usage goals they feel comfortable with and regularly revisit their log to see whether they are making progress. It may help to agree certain guidelines between the child and their parents such as 'the wi-fi gets turned off after 11pm' to enable progress. If agreeing set rules, it's important to explore possible difficulties. For example, if a student has their phone and laptop locked away after 9pm then what is their coping strategy if they are really struggling at 3am?

It's important that, as well as addressing their internet use, the student's underlying difficulties are actively addressed, if necessary with a counsellor or psychiatrist, otherwise with a trusted adult. As they begin to overcome their underlying difficulties and to develop healthier coping mechanisms, their reliance on harmful websites will naturally decrease, though it's still worth highlighting this issue with any relevant adults the student is working with so that they can build reduction of harmful internet usage into any form of recovery programme or strategy that they are currently employing.

LEARNING TO TAKE AWAY FROM THIS CHAPTER

- Internet sites and networks dedicated to self-harm and eating disorders can be both supportive and harmful. Students often inadvertently come across harmful sites when seeking support.

- Pro-ana, pro-mia and pro-harm sites see eating-disordered or self-harming behaviours as a lifestyle choice. Users share tips and ideas with each other and harmful behaviours are accepted, encouraged and promoted.

- Educating students about self-harm and eating disorders, safe sources of support and the dangers of pro-sites may decrease the likelihood of them using harmful sites.

- It can be dangerous to suddenly withdraw a student's access to harmful sites and networks which may form a support mechanism for them. Instead we need to work with them to effect a change gradually.

THINGS TO DO

- Consider how you can promote safe sources of support to your students.

- Think about whether you could or should be teaching your students about the dangers of pro-sites.

- Consider holding an ideas and information-sharing session for parents about keeping their children safe online, including information about pro-sites.

- Have pro-sites added to the blocked list on your school's web filter.

CHAPTER 14

Providing One-to-One Support

This chapter will enable you to:

- understand the role specialist school staff can play in supporting students recovering from self-harm or eating disorders to complement/ build upon any external support they receive

- develop recovery action plans for students in your care

- employ specific techniques to help students feel comfortable enough to talk openly about their difficulties

- help students to develop new, safer ways to express their emotions

- support students in turning to healthy coping mechanisms during vulnerable moments.

It can be highly beneficial to a student suffering from self-harm or an eating disorder to receive one-to-one support from a member of school staff. This may be in addition to support from an external agency, whilst on a waiting list for external support or when treatment has been completed and the student is entering the process of long-term recovery.

There are a wide range of staff who may fulfil this role, ranging from form tutors to house parents to sports coaches or school nurses or counsellors. The student will often gravitate towards a particular member of staff as someone they trust and feel comfortable talking to. If this is a member of staff who has no expertise or experience in counselling, then they are still able to provide valuable support, simply by providing the student with a safe environment to begin to explore their concerns. There are a range of ideas shared in Chapters 7 and 8 which will be particularly relevant to non-specialist staff who want to provide students causing concern with listening support and a safe environment for sharing.

More advanced recovery work should be undertaken by specialized staff who have experience and training in providing this type of support to students. This will often be a school counsellor or a member of staff whose primary role concerns student welfare. It should not be assumed that such staff have the expertise to support students in overcoming self-harm or eating disorders and regular training should be provided to ensure that they are able to carry out this role safely and confidently; if they don't, such training should be sought. The school should also ensure that any individual undertaking such work has professional indemnity insurance, either personally or through a school policy.

Most of this chapter focuses on the support that can be offered to students at school by a more specialist member of staff. The chapter is not intended to take the place of face-to-face training on the topic but rather to complement such training and to provide a range of ideas that can be turned to when working with individual students. It's also important to remember that the school should not be supporting a student in isolation. Where external agencies are involved, their guidance and advice should be sought and followed as to how best to support the student. The school should also make an active effort to engage with parents. A child's chance of recovery hugely increases when those who care for them, including their parents, the school and external agencies, work together to support them. Further ideas about working with parents and external agencies can be found in Chapters 9, 10 and 11.

The role of the school

School staff are often able to offer sustainable support when specialists aren't and also have the benefit of having an existing relationship with the student and a long-term investment in their future. The combination of external support from a specialist backed up by the school and parents is a most powerful one, especially where the school and parents are able to seek advice from, and actively work with, any specialists involved in the child's recovery. Students may require additional support between scheduled specialist therapy sessions in order to help them through the week or to help them apply what they have learned during therapy within the context of school. Again, this should be planned with the therapists to ensure it complements their work.

Due to budgetary constraints, it is relatively common for students to receive short courses of specialist treatment which end just as recovery is beginning. Preferably with input and guidance from the specialists who've been working with them, the school can continue work with the student on their recovery. We can often be guilty of assuming that once a student is weight-restored or no longer self-harming, they are no longer in need of help, but ongoing support is still vitally important. With the right infrastructure and training for staff, schools can provide that support.

'They fed me up and made me fat, ugly and miserable and gave me 18 sessions with this awful woman. Then they were like "Ta da! You're fixed." I was so not fixed, I was as miserable as I'd ever been, in fact MORE miserable because now I was fat as well. Without the help at school I'd have just gone straight back to my old tricks almost immediately.'

'I didn't realize how much my injuries conveyed to other people about how I was feeling until I stopped cutting. Once the wounds had healed and the scars started to fade, most people thought I was okay. It was hard though because I no longer had the one thing I'd always relied on to keep me calm. I was grateful for the support I continued to receive at that time, it helped me really solidify and live my recovery.'

A STUDENT SHOULD ALWAYS BE REFERRED FOR SPECIALIST SUPPORT IN THE FOLLOWING SITUATIONS

- You think the student may have suicidal feelings.

- They have attempted suicide or talked about a suicide plan.

- Their self-harm is so severe that it is putting their physical health in danger.

- You think they may have a diagnosable eating disorder.

- Symptoms have developed very rapidly and the situation is not stabilizing.

- The student has been, or is being, neglected or abused.

- You think the difficulties were triggered by a significant trauma that the child may need help coming to terms with (e.g. rape, witnessing the death of a loved one, etc.).

- You think the student poses a significant risk to themselves or others by remaining in school.

- You have tried to support the student at school but have tried all interventions available to you and the situation is not improving/has got worse.

The role of the school will be different in every instance but, as a general rule, specialist services provide intensive, highly specialized support to the student in the short term. The school can act as a bridge between sessions and go on to use the foundations laid down by specialist support as a basis for supporting medium-term recovery following treatment, especially with regard to helping the students to resume day-to-day activities and relationships. Parents can work alongside the school during this transition and go on to provide the lifelong support, love and care which will help to prevent the student from revisiting unhelpful behaviours in the future.

Looking after staff wellbeing

Providing one-to-one support to a student can be very worthwhile but very stressful and emotionally draining. In a professional therapy or counselling setting, staff receive regular supervision and opportunities to reflect on their case load. This is an important part of maintaining their wellbeing and enabling them to continue to work at their best. This kind of approach is well worth adopting at school too – both to ensure the emotional wellbeing of staff and also to allow reflection on how best to support the students who need most support. Having a chance to stop and think about a particular student without too many time pressures and with the support of experienced colleagues can be a great catalyst for working out next steps. This type of reflective practice can contribute more broadly to your school or college's ability to support students' emotional and mental health. It can either be led by a member of staff who has received specific training or by an external facilitator. Talking to your local child and adolescent mental health team or child protection team may help you recruit somebody with skills in this area who can facilitate sessions at your school.

Creating an environment for talking

It's important to create the right environment for talking to students. You need to ensure that they feel comfortable and able to talk. Think about the layout of the room – is it open and friendly? Think about having a few prompts to hand which might help to get kids talking. I find play dough, and a few board games, some pens and paper and a few magazines are a good start. I also make sure that a student is comfortable and, if they would like to, I am happy for them to eat snacks or have a hot or cold drink when we talk. I try to provide the drinks and snacks once I know their preference to make the sessions feel welcoming.

Your first session will often be fairly loose, whilst you and the student become more comfortable talking to each other and you begin to understand what each of you is hoping to get from the sessions. This is a great time to establish any ground rules and set the tone for all future conversations. You might want to agree things like:

- if there is any information that needs to be passed on, you will discuss with the student who needs to know, what they need to know and why (in line with the school's policies and procedures with regard to confidentiality)

- what the student should call you – within this setting and around school if this is different

- what they can expect from you, for example you will be there, on time, ready to listen, you will not judge or dismiss and you will offer practical support where possible

- (perhaps) what you can expect of them in return.

Don't get too carried away though, the first session may be quite short and is really just to offer reassurance to the student. Every care should be taken not to scare them off at this early stage.

Developing a recovery action plan

If you're trying to help a student overcome their self-harm or eating-disordered behaviours, it can be helpful to have a plan in place. This doesn't need to be long-winded or overly technical, but really just a way to help you to solidify your aims, decide what you're going to do and to make sure that all the appropriate people are kept in the loop.

I would recommend creating plans with short- to medium-term aims, so that they are realistic and achievable and you and the student are able to see progress. Each time an aim is achieved I would write a new plan. Working through the plan either with the student or with colleagues can be a very useful exercise in itself and having one clear focus of your work with a student can also be helpful in enabling you to find a direction and purpose for your sessions.

Exactly what this plan should entail will depend on your preferences and what stage you're at with the student. I've outlined below some things you might want to consider when creating an action plan.

What is your aim?

Consider your key concerns and what you hope to achieve. You might be hoping to get a student to make an initial disclosure, or to support them in reducing the frequency of their self-harm or to attend the lunch hall for a meal. Have a clear aim and don't try to achieve too much with each plan. You can always start the process again when things move on.

It can also be helpful to think about what might happen if you don't put support in place in order to work out what your key aim is. When you think about it that way, you might find that your key aim is to keep a student in school, for example.

How will you measure success and track progress?

Think about what will be different if you succeed with your aim, or are making progress towards it. What changes in behaviour might you be able to see and how might you measure them? It might be that a student willingly engages in a supportive conversation for 15 minutes, or that they manage to go without harming for 24 hours. It will be different for each individual so you need to tailor the plan to their situation.

It's important to track progress, otherwise both you and the student will feel like you're not making any progress. Consider what information you should record and how you might chart progress – you might consider including information about school absence, frequency of harming behaviour or where the student reports themselves to be on an anxiety scale (where 1 = completely calm and 10 = so anxious that they cannot continue with daily activities).

What can you do?

Again, with the specific student in mind, think carefully about exactly what you'll do in order to support them. There is lots you can do, from organizing a bolt hole for them at school to go to if they feel anxious, to discussing alternative behaviours they can carry out when they feel a need to harm, to organizing regular times to sit down and offer face-to-face support, to encouraging them to keep a journal.

Things you need to consider specifically when planning what to do include:

- *What* – what activities will help you to achieve your aim? Consider whether you have access to the resources required, and if not, how you might overcome this hurdle.

- *Who* – who else might you need to involve or inform about your plan?

- *When* – when do you hope to get started? How long do you think it will take to achieve your aim? Are there any specific timeframes you need to work around, such as upcoming holidays or exams? Think carefully about whether you're being realistic in your time planning. Overcoming eating-disordered or self-harming thoughts and behaviours is not usually a quick win.

Feedback loop
Be sure to revisit your plan regularly and to allow it to evolve to reflect what is and isn't working. Consider:

- What is working well? Why?
- What has worked less well? Why?
- What could you do differently or better?

Think about the best questions to consider and the frequency with which you should revisit and revise your plan, and stick to it. Students' needs can change quite rapidly as they enter recovery and someone who could not manage without an hour-long chat every three days one month, may respond better to regular five-minute catch-ups the next.

Think also about whether there is anyone you should be sharing this information with:

- What do you need to share?
- Who will you share it with?
- How frequently will you share the information?
- In what format will you share it?

When writing an action plan, the key thing is to ensure that it is an evolving and useful tool. It should be a basic document that helps to solidify your ideas and keep you on track. You should never be afraid to update or adapt it if it's not working and never worry about starting again.

Action plans and other sensitive information about a student should be stored securely, in line with your school's child protection policy.

Helping students feel comfortable enough to talk
Many students will find it hard to talk about how they're feeling and there are a range of different strategies that people use to alleviate this.

The most successful I have come across are using play dough and writing lists. I have outlined each of these approaches in some depth on the following pages.

Using play dough to get students talking

It might sound like a silly idea, but having a tub, or tubs, of play dough in your office can be a great way to encourage students to explore their issues and open up about their thoughts and feelings. It works well with younger students and surprisingly well with older ones too. The only real limit is your imagination, and if you start using play dough you'll probably soon discover dozens of ways of using it, but here are some ideas to get you started.

USE IT AS A SIMPLE DISTRACTION

Just having a tub of play dough to hand can act as a distraction, giving the student something to focus on other than the difficult conversation they're having. They can squeeze it and stretch it to relieve tension and many will begin to talk more freely as they play with it. Some will choose to play with it for a few minutes before they begin to talk at all. Giving them the time and space to do this will often help them to get ready to talk.

SMASH IT TO RELIEVE ANGER

If a student is feeling especially angry, making a big ball of play dough and inviting them to smash it can help them to feel a lot better and enable them to calm down enough to begin to explore how they're feeling. You might then ask questions about who or what they were thinking of as they punched the play dough.

MODEL SCENARIOS

Some students will get really carried away with using play dough and will happily use it to model scenarios, either in a very literal way or by using balls to represent different people. Some might use it to demonstrate something that has happened that they can't put into words, or to show their mood or to demonstrate things that they would like to do to somebody (like a voodoo doll). Sometimes the play dough can be used quite symbolically, to represent an idea which may not fully sink in otherwise or may need reinforcing. For example, if a student feels in danger from someone, the play dough can be used to represent that person and put them in a box, to show that you are going to take steps to ensure that they are safe from that person.

MAKE A FACE

If a student struggles to express their emotions, sometimes they may find it easier to do so with a play dough face, where they can play out expressions they may struggle with. They could also use the play dough face to explore how different things make them feel – for example, if you were talking with a student who regularly self-harmed, you could explore how they feel when they're self-harming and then how they feel after they've self-harmed to explore any differences in their emotions at these two times.

USE COLOURS TO REPRESENT MOOD

Having several colours of play dough can make for some interesting conversations as many students will find it interesting to explore their moods and emotions through colours. Another technique is to start with a blob of bright play dough, for example, red or blue, and a blob of white play dough, and ask the student to mix the colours to represent their responses to different scenarios. For instance, bright blue (with no white added) might represent their most unhappy and adding more and more white might represent a happier mood. You could use this to explore how they've felt at different points in the week, in response to different scenarios or after using different coping strategies to try and gauge their emotions. Coloured sand is an excellent alternative.

SIZE OF BALL

The size of a ball of play dough can also be used to represent a wide range of different things. For example, a big ball of play dough might be used to represent feeling very angry. You could explore different strategies for helping the student calm down which will be represented by the ball getting smaller. For each strategy you suggest, they could hand you back a corresponding part of their play dough ball; a big chunk means a strategy that will calm them down a lot whereas a small chunk represents a strategy that is less impactful. Of course, if you suggest anything which will increase rather than alleviate their anger, you'll have to pass them back some play dough to increase the size of their ball. This idea can be adapted in many different ways, for example, the ball might represent feeling safe or happy or calm.

INTERPRET AN IMAGE OF THEMSELVES

Asking a student to create an image of themselves in play dough can be an interesting exercise and you might explore with them why they've created an image of themselves in a certain way if there is anything about their creation which is open to interpretation. For example, sometimes children will add a heart so you might say, 'I see that the play dough "you" has got a heart – is that to represent that you're a kind and caring person?'

THE THIRD PERSON

Another benefit to having a student create a play dough representation of themselves is that it enables them to talk about themselves in the third person, which they will often find easier. Make it clear that the play dough person is a representation of the student you're working with (using the prefix 'Little' works well, i.e. if the student is called Tina then play dough Tina could be referred to as 'Little Tina'). Talk to the student about things that have happened to Little Tina or what Little Tina's hopes are, what makes her happy, sad, and so on. Children will often talk far more freely about the hopes and fears of 'little them' than they will when addressing the question directly in the first person.

Using lists to support students in recovery from self-harm and eating disorders

Lists can be a great way for students to communicate their thoughts and feelings when they don't have the skills or confidence to write in greater depth. They can be a good starting point for your conversations with a student about the thoughts and feelings underlying their difficulties and can be an effective way of gaining an understanding of issues that need to be explored which may feel less invasive or daunting than writing prose or poetry at length.

All of the specific lists below are potential starting points which might be extended in a variety of ways. Specific extensions to each list are given after each list type. In addition to these, general extensions always worth considering include:

WRITE A LIST OF A DIFFERENT LENGTH

Shorter lists are great if you're short of time or ideas (sometimes a short list can be the catalyst for a longer one). Conversely, a longer list can be a great way to drive home a point. Working with a student to think up 25 things which they have achieved and can feel proud of, for instance, can be very self-affirming.

CHOOSE A SPECIFIC TIMEFRAME

Set the list in the context of time. Apply it to this morning, or the last week or the next month for instance.

CHOOSE A SPECIFIC LOCATION

Set the list in the context of a specific location, home or school, for example. It can often be a very interesting exercise to write the same list with reference to different places. For example, 'Ten things that make me angry at school' may shape up very differently to 'Ten things that make me angry at home'.

CHOOSE A SPECIFIC PERSON

Write the list with a specific person in mind. This will most likely be a friend or a family member but sometimes you might want to look at things through the eyes of an imagined other or the student you're working with, but in the past or the future.

Specific list ideas

Once you get started, you'll think of many more, but here are three worked through in depth to get you started.

TEN THINGS THAT MAKE ME ANGRY

Ask the student you're working with to write a list of ten things that make them angry. You can learn a lot by exploring this list openly with them. Ask them open questions about why the different items on the list cause them to feel angry and explore the different types of anger they might feel towards the different items on the list. You might also consider ranking the list with the student, thinking about which things make them most angry and why that is.

Once the student is a little more comfortable talking about their self-harm you might reframe the list to make it specifically refer to things that made them so angry that they have caused themselves harm, or they've carried out unhealthy food-related behaviours such as bingeing, restricting or purging. This can be a good way to understand specific triggers for their behaviours; you can then explore how these triggers might be avoided in the future.

Possible extensions

- Five things that make me angry

- Twenty-five things that make me angry

- Ten things that made me angry this week

- Three things that made me angry today

- Ten things at school that make me angry

- Ten things at home that make me angry

- Ten things that my best friend does that make me angry

- Ten things that my brother/sister/parent does that make me angry

- Ten things that made me so angry I hurt myself

TEN THINGS THAT MAKE ME FEEL CALM

At the moment when a student feels overcome with emotion and the need to harm themselves or carry out unhealthy food-related behaviours, it can be very difficult for them to think of anything beyond their turmoil of emotions and the urge to cause themselves harm. Taking time to explore different things that make them feel calm at a time when they are not feeling the urge to self-harm can be a good way of helping them to develop coping techniques for more difficult times.

For each item on the list consider why it makes them feel calm. Keep an eye out for anything in the list which could be adapted to form a coping strategy which can be incorporated into everyday life without being noticed. For instance, if a student listed 'playing with my cat' as something that made them feel calm, you could explore whether remembering the last time they played with their cat, or looking at a picture of their cat, helps them to feel calm as these are both things they can easily do even when they're not able to access their cat directly.

Talk about what feeling calm feels like and why it's a good way to try and feel when the urge to self-harm comes about. You might also consider using this opportunity to talk about more general calming strategies such as deep, slow breathing, emptying their mind and purposefully relaxing each part of their body.

Possible extensions

- Five things that make me calm

- Twenty-five things that make me calm

- Ten things that helped me calm down this week

- Three things that made me feel more calm today

- Ten things that can help me calm down at school

- Ten things that can help me calm down at home

- Ten ways my friends can help me to feel calm

- Ten things that my brother/sister/parent does that make me calmer

- Five ways I have used to calm myself down when I felt an urge to self-harm

THREE PEOPLE I CAN TALK TO WHEN I'M IN NEED OF SUPPORT

Helping students identify people they can talk to is a really helpful activity. You might want to qualify the list as you may sometimes specifically want to talk about people the student feels they can talk to in relation to their self-harm or eating disorder, whilst other times you may want to discuss people that they feel they can talk to for more general support, or just to get their feelings off their chest.

When you explore their list with them, it's important to discuss the issues of boundaries and think about what it is appropriate to talk about with whom. For example, there are some discussions which should always be saved for a trusted adult rather than shared with a friend who may not know how to respond and may find it very difficult to support without getting upset themselves. You might suggest different people to go on the list, from the school counsellor, to someone at home, to friends or trusted adults at school. Some students will also find they can talk to someone on a helpline or may even list a pet. You might also want to explore the concept of talking as it can be usefully interpreted more broadly to mean openly sharing via, for example, email or an online forum as well as actually vocalizing their feelings. This might cause the list to look a little different.

To ensure that a student has the support that they need both during school hours and also at weekends and during holidays, you might specifically want to identify who they can talk to when they're at school and when they're at home. If a student is in their final year at school, you may also want to start exploring support networks they can access as they transition into the next stage of their life.

Possible extensions

- Five people I can talk to when I'm in need of support

- Three people I've talked to in the past who've helped me when I needed support

- Three people who I think would be supportive but I've not tried talking to yet

- Three people I can talk to when I'm in need of support at school

- Three people I can talk to when I'm in need of support at the weekend

- Three people I could talk to when I'm in need of support at university

- Three people/helplines I could talk to when I'm in need of support at 3am

- Three places I can go online when I'm in need of support

Other examples of lists that could work include 'Five things that make me feel more in control', 'Five things I'm proud of' or 'Three things I'm looking forward to'. Once you start working with a student, you'll begin to get a feel for what will work best with them – follow your gut and utilize the surprising power of lists to support you.

Developing new ways to express emotions

For many students who have unhealthy thoughts and behaviours around self-harm, eating and food, they have no alternative way of expressing and managing their emotions. A key part of your role can be to help them to work towards developing new ways of expressing themselves.

The best way to do this is to get to know and understand the student as well as you can so that you can help them to tap in to the skills and characteristics that they may be able to utilize to help them better manage their emotions. This might tap into their skills with writing, art, music, drama, athletics and so on. The plan for each individual will be absolutely tailored to that individual. Two of the common methods for exploring emotions within sessions which tend to work well with a cross section of students are the use of writing and the use of art. I've provided a few examples below, though there are whole texts on these topics.

Using writing

Writing can be a powerful way for a student to chart their recovery process. Depending on how writing is used, it may mean they end up with a record of the journey they have come on which can help to highlight just how far they have come. In addition to using lists (see above), the following strategies are popular and useful:

JOURNALLING

Journalling can be done in a manner of different ways. A student may keep a perfunctory journal which helps to chart the highs and lows of the week and can help to isolate triggers for changes in thoughts, feelings or behaviours. This type of journal is one a student will often share in sessions. On the other hand, many students may choose to chart their personal journey by recording very private thoughts and feelings that they may not be happy to share. Sometimes students will happily share snippets of their journal, but even if they don't then the act of writing down how they are feeling can be quite therapeutic and useful for them to revisit later. Some students will also gain a lot from reading and discussing memoirs by other people who've recovered from similar issues.

POETRY

Poetry can be a powerful tool. As well as reading the poems of others who have suffered from self-harm and eating disorders, if students can gain enough confidence to write their own poems, this can be very therapeutic and a fantastic starting point for conversations.

STORYTELLING

Storytelling can be used to explore a student's thoughts and feelings by projecting them onto others. Students will find it less intimidating to tell a fictional story about characters than to explore their own feelings. But exploring the feelings of others can be a good way to begin to understand and explore our own feelings and to understand how our behaviours may impact on others too. The easiest routes into storytelling are either to provide a prompt, title or first line, or to decide to retell a well-known story, such as a fairy tale, in the future or in the present day.

Using art

Art can be a very powerful tool for exploring and expressing emotions. Some of the simplest ways that you might use art in a session are:

CREATING SOMETHING EXPRESSIVE

The aim is to create a drawing, painting or sculpture which represents the way the student feels, or the person or thing who is making them angry; essentially the end product is the focus. There will be lots of discussion along the way about how creating the piece is making them feel, why they've chosen certain textures and colours and so forth. Each little detail is likely to reveal something new if you take the time to explore.

ENABLING EXPRESSION THROUGH THE ART OF CREATING

Simply working with artistic tools and materials can be highly soothing and therapeutic. Sculpting or moulding clay, mixing paint or creating abstract walls of colour, regardless of the product, can help a student to work through their feelings on a topic.

CREATING SOMETHING TO DESTROY

If a student is especially angry or upset by something or someone, creating a related art piece of any kind that they can then destroy in order to release and let go of those feelings can be a helpful strategy for moving forwards. They might tear up a drawing or smash a sculpture or black out a painting; either way they are likely to find the process relieves them of many feelings and leaves them more free to explore their underlying tensions with you.

Alternatives to unhealthy behaviours

In addition to helping students to express themselves within the safe and therapeutic environment we create for them at school, we also need to enable them to manage their feelings when they are alone. There are lots and lots of different ideas that students might try. The following few pages contain over 130 different strategies you could discuss with students in your care, categorized by the reason they need to find a coping mechanism at that moment. They are written to be shared directly with students who have a need to access healthier coping strategies. Some of them sound a little strange, but they've all been suggested by students recovering from self-harm or eating-disordered behaviours.

One way of using them is to work with a student to generate a list of ideas they will try when they feel unable to cope, using the ideas below as inspiration, and encourage the student to write this list up on their smartphone, in their planner or on a card they can carry in their wallet. Then, when they find they aren't managing they can turn to their list and have immediate access to some suggested coping strategies.

Ideas that simulate self-harm

These are ideas that will give you some of the visual or physical sensation of self-harm without actually causing harm to the body.

- Ping an elastic band or hair band on your wrist (but not too hard).

- Draw red lines on your skin.

- Clench an ice cube in your hand.

- Write on your skin.

- Finger paint using red paint.

- On a photo or drawing of yourself, mark in red where you want to hurt yourself.

Ideas for when you need to vent your feelings

Sometimes our feelings become too much for us to bear and the only way we can think of managing them is to hurt ourselves or turn to food. Here are some alternatives that can help you to vent anger, frustration or other extreme feelings.

- Go somewhere quiet and scream.

- Punch a punch bag.

- Make a ball out of play dough and smash it.

- Hurl lumps of ice at the ground and watch them smash.

- Smash a watermelon.

- Hammer nails into wood.

- Play squash.

- Tear up a magazine.

- Write down what made you feel angry and scribble it out until the paper is worn through.

- Dance like nobody is watching.

- Play music loudly.

- Bang drums or other percussion instruments.

- Run up a hill.

- Write a letter to the person who has made you angry, venting your frustration (but don't send it).

- Cry.

- Cut up an old piece of material.

- Tear up cardboard.

- Have a pillow fight with a wall.

- Stamp your feet.

- Snap sticks in half.

- Sing very loudly.

Ideas for when you feel alone or down

These are ideas which will help when your mood is low; when you feel alone or deeply sad and you don't know why.

- Look at photographs of your friends and family.

- Think of your favourite day ever.

- Tell someone about your favourite day ever.

- Talk to someone you trust.

- Call a helpline or use an online forum.

- Listen to soothing music.

- Take a walk in the garden, notice each tree and flower and try to learn their names.

- Walk your dog.

- Go to the park and swing. Listen to the laughter of children and let it infect you.

- Reread your favourite childhood book.

- Watch silly videos of cats on YouTube.

Ideas to help you feel more in control

If everything feels out of control and the urge to self-harm or turn to unhealthy food behaviours is because we feel like we need to control something, these ideas can help instead:

- Put your books in height, alphabetical or colour order.

- Plan your diary for the next week; build in rest or fun breaks.

- Build something intricate like an Airfix or LEGO® model.

- Paint by numbers.

- Read a kids' 'choose your own adventure' book making all the 'wrong' choices.

- Make bread from scratch.

- Give your bedroom a facelift by shifting the furniture around.

- Give your room a deep clean.

Delaying tactics to give you a short time to think
When you're trying hard to give up self-harming, bingeing or purging, sometimes you know that if you can just give yourself a little time to think then you'll be able to reason with yourself. These ideas will buy you a minute or two to try and calm your anxiety and remind yourself of safer coping mechanisms (you might do one of these before going on to try one of the ideas in another category).

- Set a timer on your phone for 60 seconds and watch it tick down before you do anything.

- Recite the alphabet forwards and then backwards.

- Practise your times tables.

- Take the item you intend to harm with and wrap it up in towels, blankets or newspaper.

- Count to 100.

- Sing 'Twinkle, Twinkle, Little Star'.

- Run up and down stairs three times.

Ideas for when you need a distraction
Sometimes the need to self-harm, binge, purge or exercise is less intense but it doesn't go away that fast and you need something to take your mind off it for a little longer. These ideas might help. If you regularly turn to unhealthy coping mechanisms at the same time each day, you might also find that these are good activities to do at that time to help you avoid carrying out harmful behaviours.

- Watch something light-hearted on TV.

- Go for a walk.

- Call your best friend for a chat.

- Have a shower.

- Do a jigsaw.

- Go on an alphabet hunt – try to find something beginning with every letter of the alphabet.

- Write a letter or an email.

- Read a book.

- Sleep.

- Learn the words to a new song.

- Practise a musical instrument.

- Curl up on a bean bag and watch the world go by.

- Play a computer game.

- Juggle.

- Practise a new skill (e.g. speaking a language, juggling).

- Bake.

- Sew or knit.

- Build a card house or line of cards then knock it down.

- Look for pictures in the clouds.

- Do some cleaning.

- Work in the garden: dead-head some flowers or do some weeding.

- Fly a kite.

- Watch out for birds and try to identify the different types.

- Skim stones – how many bounces can you do?

- Dig for worms.

- Write a blog post or journal entry.

Ideas for when you're confused

Sometimes our thoughts get all muddled and we don't know what to think. These are ideas that can help us to start thinking a little more straight and begin to understand ourselves and what is going on around us.

- Write a poem called 'I don't understand'.

- Paint a big, abstract, picture using poster paints.

- Write a list of questions you wish you knew the answer to (you could share them with someone later).

- Stop and work backwards through the last hour trying to answer the question 'What made me feel this way?'

- Ask yourself what would the blade/flame, etc. say to me if it could talk?

- Express yourself through music, art or words.

- Trace each of your scars with your finger and remember the story it tells.

Ideas for the middle of the night

The middle of the night can feel like a very lonely time when it can be hard to use our normal coping strategies. There are a few things you can try though:

- Call a 24-hour helpline.

- Write down how you're feeling with the aim of sharing it with a trusted adult in the morning.

- Make yourself a warm drink and drink it slowly.

- Look for constellations in the night sky.

- Talk to friends online who are in different time zones.

- Look through old photo albums.

Ideas that won't be noticed in busy situations

When the urge to self-harm or binge overcomes you in the middle of a crowded situation or in a lesson, it can be hard to know what to do to manage how you're feeling. Here are a few ideas that nobody will even know you're doing:

- Scream silently in your head.

- Imagine yourself in your favourite place with your favourite people.

- Become aware of every part of your body in turn: think about your toes, then your ankles, then your knees, and so on.

- Breathe deeply and slowly, counting to five with each inhalation and each exhalation.

- Recite a fact about each other person in the room in your head.

- If you're amongst strangers, pick one and imagine what they did last Friday.

- Put your hands in your pockets and pinch your thighs.

Ideas that nurture rather than harm

Sometimes, doing something which involves caring for something or someone else can be the perfect antidote to feelings of self-harm.

- Water the garden.

- Feed or brush a pet.

- Play with a sibling.

- Sing to a baby.

- Write a message to say thank you to a friend or family member for something kind they have done.

- Plan what you will buy your family for Christmas.

- Massage the part of your body that you feel the urge to harm.

- Look after your older wounds or scars, clean them and dress them.

- Ask someone you care about for a hug.

- Smooth body lotion into the places you want to harm.

- Rub Bio-Oil into your old scars.

- Put on your cosiest, biggest jumper and give yourself a hug.

Ideas that remind you that you're real

On some occasions, the chief reason that we feel the need to self-harm is just to remind ourselves that we're real, to prevent the feeling of numbness from overtaking us. If that's how you're feeling, these ideas might help:

- Google yourself.

- Read your last school report.

- Paint your finger and toe nails.

- Have a cold shower.

- Ask someone to give you a massage.

- Punch a cushion.

- Plunge your hands into a bowl of ice water.

- Eat an ice lolly (popsicle); focus on how the cold feels on your tongue.

- Eat spicy food.

- Have a water fight with a friend or sibling.

- Smell different spices and really focus on the smell.

- Try to remember every birthday cake you've ever had.

- Read old blog posts or diary entries.

- Read your first school report and remember yourself as a five-year-old.

Ideas that remind you that you have a future

The future can feel like an unreal prospect at times and all we can think of is the desperate thoughts and feelings we're experiencing now. Sometimes, casting our minds forwards can be a helpful way to enable ourselves to find our way out of the emotional difficulties we're facing in the here and now.

- Plan your ultimate 21st birthday party.

- If you have exams coming up, think about how you'll feel on your last day of exams.

- Imagine who you'll be friends with when you're 30.

- Plan the speech you'll give at your 100th birthday.

- Think about the three things you most hope to achieve in life.

- Write your bucket list.

Ideas that help you to understand and celebrate yourself

When we feel a need to self-harm, it's often accompanied by a feeling of utter worthlessness. We think there is nothing unique or special about us, that no one could ever love or care for us and that we're taking up space unnecessarily. Taking some time to learn to understand our strengths and unique characteristics and abilities better can help us to realize that we're not so worthless after all.

- Make a collage of all the things you most enjoy.

- Recall your proudest moment and the many steps that led up to it.

- Imagine what your closest friend would say if someone asked them to describe you.

- Write a list of five things you'd like to do in the next year.

- Write a list of the five funniest or most special things that have happened in the last year.

- Ask yourself 'How do I feel? Am I angry? Am I anxious? Why?'

- Draw yourself as your friend or sibling sees you.

- Imagine what the soundtrack to the film of your life would be.

LEARNING TO TAKE AWAY FROM THIS CHAPTER

- School staff can play an important role in the recovery of students.

- Supporting students can be stressful for school staff and put their wellbeing at risk if they are not appropriately supported.

- Developing action recovery plans featuring realistic aims can help to keep us focused on a student's recovery and enable us to see the progress we are making.

- Lists and play dough can both be used to help get students talking.

- There are simple ways of supporting students to safely express difficult emotions through writing or art.

- Sharing ideas with students about safe ways to manage their feelings at moments when they feel the urge to turn to unhealthy behaviours can help them to reduce their reliance on unhealthy behaviours.

THINGS TO DO

- Think about how you can ensure the wellbeing of staff who support student recovery from self-harm and eating disorders.

- Create a simple form you can use for recording and sharing student recovery plans.

- Buy some play dough, pads and pens.

- Work with students currently in your care to develop lists of alternative behaviours they can turn to when they feel an urge to hurt themselves.

CHAPTER 15

Motivational Interviewing as a Tool for Behaviour Change

This chapter will enable you to:

- understand what motivational interviewing is and how it can be used to elicit behaviour change

- use open questions, affirmations, reflective listening and summary statements when supporting students

- apply motivational interviewing techniques to develop discrepancy, express empathy, amplify ambivalence, roll with resistance and support self-efficacy when working with students.

Motivational interviewing is a technique used by counsellors and therapists working with people with a variety of behaviours which are resistant to change, including drug and alcohol abuse and eating disorders. In short, it is a way of talking to people that helps them to understand and embrace the need to change. It helps them to become a proactive part of that change and helps to prevent a situation where you are constantly offering advice, only for it to be ignored. It is a technique that is simple to get started with but takes practice to master. This chapter is designed to give you an overview and some ideas to practise with. You'll find it helpful when working with students who suffer from self-harming or eating-disordered behaviours as well as more generally in your role at school.

Anyone who's ever worked with adolescents knows that the more you ask, tell or plead with them to do something that they're not inclined to do, the less and less likely they become to do it. So however desperately you might want to help an anorexic teenager who's fading away before your eyes, begging them to eat something simply isn't going to prove effective. Often it will have the opposite effect and encourage them to stick more steadfastly to their rigid rules. This doesn't just apply to food of course – the response would be the same if we were talking about self-harm or homework…

This is where motivational interviewing comes in. This is a method that is designed to elicit a behavioural change in people who do not recognize the need for change, or feel ambivalent about it or cannot work out for themselves how to effect change. The technique is successful because it puts the student in control of their own recovery. You act as a facilitator, helping them to explore their feelings and different potential outcomes but never telling them what to do. Instead, with your support, the student finds their own path to change and is therefore far more likely to stick to it.

The spirit of motivational interviewing

There are four basic skills involved in motivational interviewing. These are useful skills that can be adapted to almost any situation and may prove most useful more generally in the classroom as well as when working with vulnerable students. Developing and using these skills will help you to become a better listener, help you to better understand the person you're working with, help you to help them to determine appropriate goals for behaviour change and help you to help motivate them to change their current behaviour to meet these goals.

The four basic motivational interviewing skills can be remembered using the acronym 'OARS':

Open questions

Affirmations

Reflective listening

Summary statements.

Open questions
An open question is one that requires a relatively extensive response – that is, it can't be answered in a word or two, such as 'yes', 'no', 'nine', 'next week' and so on. Asking open questions invites people to talk and explore their ideas. This is a great way of helping us to understand more about the person we're talking to, and allowing them to give a fuller response can often lead to them exploring their thoughts and feelings surrounding difficult issues in a way that a closed question never could.

Open question examples:

- Who is important to you in your life and why?

- How can we help you to…?

- What was the best/worst five minutes of your day?

- What do you want to do next?

- What do you know about the risks of regularly making yourself sick?

- How do your self-harming behaviours affect your relationships with your friends/family?

Affirmations

Making affirming statements helps individuals acknowledge their positive behaviours and strengths, which then builds their confidence in their ability to change. Affirming statements allow both for recognition of their difficulties and for support of their strengths, letting them know that their concerns and issues are valid. These affirmations convey respect, understanding and support and need to be both genuine and appropriate.

Examples of affirmations:

- You're clearly very resourceful.

- You handled yourself really well in a difficult situation.

- That's a great idea.

- If I were in your shoes, I'm not sure I could manage nearly as well as you.

- You're trying really hard.

Reflective listening

You can show that you're really listening and understanding what is being said by paraphrasing someone's comments and repeating them back. This has the benefit of proving that you're listening, whilst reaffirming for the individual what they have said – this is especially important if it is about changing their behaviour. This technique will also mean you'll quickly clear up anything you've not fully understood.

Reflective listening examples:

- So you think that...

- It sounds as if you...

- You're wondering if...

- So, what I think you're saying is...

- Please correct me if I'm wrong, but what I think you mean is...

Summary statements

Summary statements pull together everything stated and are much like the types of statements you would use to demonstrate reflective listening, but more overarching as you pull together the salient themes and ideas from a whole conversation. Again, this helps to reaffirm what has been said, to ensure that you fully understand the individual's thoughts, desires and intentions and can also act as a good bridge before moving onto a new topic or ending the conversation for the day.

Summary statement examples:

- Let me see if I understand this so far...

- Tell me if I miss anything...so in summary...

- We've covered a lot of ground today...

- Would you agree that the most important things we've talked about today are...?

- You must be exhausted, we've talked about a lot...

Principles of motivational interviewing

Motivational interviewing is based around five principles, easily remembered using the acronym 'DEARS':

Develop discrepancy

Express empathy

Amplify ambivalence

Roll with resistance

Support self-efficacy.

Developing discrepancy

The aim of developing discrepancy is to help the student to realize that there is a difference between where they currently are and where they want to be, and that their current behaviour is standing in the way of some of their goals. The goal is to motivate the student to resolve the discrepancy by changing their behaviour.

Developing discrepancy examples:

- What are the good things, and the not so good things about restricting your calorie intake?

- How do you think your life would be different if you didn't self-harm?

- You say that your studies are important to you, but not eating is preventing you from doing so well; help me to understand which is more important to you…

- How will things be in a year from now if you continue to self-harm?

- Hypothetically speaking, if you were to make a change in any area of your life, what would it be?

Expressing empathy

Students suffering with self-harming or eating-disordered behaviours will often feel terrified, and very alone. They will feel like no one in the world could possibly understand them except, perhaps, a fellow sufferer. Most people don't even try to understand, dismissing their behaviour as ridiculous, harmful and something that must change. By stepping into the shoes of a sufferer and trying to understand why they are behaving in a particular way, you will gain a far better picture of how you can support. You will also go a long way towards earning the trust of the student concerned.

Expressing empathy examples:

- I understand this must be really difficult.

- You must feel so confused about what to do.

- I can imagine you must feel very angry and confused right now.

- I know you're trying and you're finding it really hard.

- I understand that the thought of eating more is terrifying.

Amplifying ambivalence

Even the sufferers who are most reluctant or unable to address and change their eating or self-harming behaviours tend to recognize some negatives of their difficulties. These might be minor or fleeting, so our job is to seize them, repeat them and magnify them in order to help the sufferer begin to understand that there are two sides to this story; that their unhealthy behaviours are not a perfect haven. Encouraging students to explore the negatives as well as the positives about their situation can help them to recognize that change might have some positive outcomes.

Amplifying ambivalence examples:

- Has your self-harm caused concern to your friends or family?

- What happens when your friends get together for a meal out – can you join in?

- What was your life like before you started self-harming?

- If you keep heading down the road you're on, where do you see it ending?

- Isn't it hard to focus on your schoolwork when you're preoccupied with food all the time?

Rolling with resistance

Even if on some level they want to change, students who've been relying on unhealthy coping mechanisms for some time can be very resistant to the idea of change. You may feel like you're making progress only to find that after one step forwards it's two steps back and the student concerned is adamant that they want things to stay just as they are for a little longer because that feels more manageable and safer to them. The key here is not to damage the good relationship you've been developing by lecturing, pestering, badgering or otherwise insisting on change. As difficult as it is, you have to allow the student to take control and let you know when they're ready to move forwards. This means accepting and allowing their resistance to change. The next step is to explore it to see how it can be overcome.

Rolling with resistance examples:

- That's okay, if you're not ready yet, we can come back to it.

- It sounds like maybe you don't feel quite sure about all this right now?

- What would you like to do now? How would you like to proceed?

- I understand – what would you like to do next?

- Would you prefer if we talked about something different for a while?

Supporting self-efficacy

This process is all about enabling a student to take control of their own destiny; they create their own goals and, with support, they find the best path towards those goals. The path won't always be smooth and linear but the important thing is that they keep trying and that they are given clear and positive support each and every time they come up with a suggestion for making a change, no matter how small. You can support verbally and also physically by helping the plan to be realized, if it's beyond the reach or remit of the student.

Supporting self-efficacy examples:

- You've clearly thought long and hard about this.

- This sounds like a great idea, how can we make it happen?

- Yes, you've slipped up on a couple of these things but you've had great success with…

- You've clearly made some real progress – how are you feeling about that?

- You must feel proud of yourself, that was quite a hurdle you've overcome this week.

Applying motivational interviewing at school

This probably seems like quite a lot to take in – and in truth it's a skill that can take people many years to master, but it's such a great technique for working with students that I thought it was well worth sharing the basics with you.

The best way to really get to grips with motivational interviewing is to practise, practise, practise. You don't need to wait until you've got a student with eating disorder or self-harming behaviours to practise on; you're surrounded by students every day, and I'm sure that their behaviours aren't always what you'd want or hope for, so a simple exercise you can do to practise your motivational interviewing skills is to pick a behaviour you'd like to change in the students you work with and see if you can encourage students to *want* to change it by using the motivational interviewing techniques shared in this chapter. Perhaps you'd like to see everyone wearing correct uniform, or to settle down to learn more quickly at the beginning of the lesson, or to complete their homework on time. Take something relatively simple and think about how you can use motivational interviewing skills to alter that behaviour either in one student, or a whole class if you're feeling brave.

LEARNING TO TAKE AWAY FROM THIS CHAPTER

- Students whose self-harming or eating-disordered thoughts and behaviours have persisted for some time may be resistant to the idea of change.

- Motivational interviewing is a widely used way of motivating people to want to change and works well with students struggling to overcome self-harm or eating disorders.

- When you use motivational interviewing techniques, you put the student at the heart of their own recovery and increase the likelihood of sustainable changes in behaviour.

- You don't have to wait until you're working with a vulnerable student to practise motivational interviewing techniques; you can use it in day-to-day life too.

THINGS TO DO

- Think about simple changes you can make to the way you interact with students in your care which will bring your communications more in line with motivational interviewing techniques. For example, can you use more open questions, or make use of summary statements or affirmations?

- Practise your motivational interviewing skills by choosing a low-stake behaviour to try to change. Can you motivate your students to arrive on time for lessons, for example?

CHAPTER 16

The Road to Recovery

This chapter will enable you to:

- understand that recovery is not always linear or perfect – and that's okay

- recognize and manage blips during recovery

- celebrate recovery in its many forms.

Many people wonder about whether it's possible to recover from self-harm or an eating disorder and opinion is definitely divided. I think that so long as students learn to recognize their triggers, adopt healthier coping mechanisms and understand how to utilize their support networks, both short- and long-term recovery are possible. It's not always perfect – and that's important to remember as many perfectionist students will be disappointed with anything other than a perfect recovery – but this is simply unrealistic.

Blips during eating disorder recovery

Recovery is usually neither straightforward nor perfect, and learning to overcome short-term setbacks is an important part of the long-term recovery process for students overcoming self-harm and eating disorders. In particular students may need additional support to overcome the following:

Relapse

Recovery can feel very much like two steps forwards and one step back. It's not uncommon for a student who had previously been recovering well to turn to self-harming or eating-disordered behaviour again. You should expect this and keep an eye out for the warning signs and make sure that the student has access to someone they feel they can talk to.

Whilst the student is in recovery, before relapse occurs, or between relapses, you can talk to them about the possibility of relapses and agree a strategy for dealing with them. Whilst the student is in a positive mindset and a period of positive recovery they are likely to be able to give you some very good ideas about how to support them during a more difficult period.

A different eating disorder

One of the largest risk factors for developing an eating disorder is having suffered from an eating disorder in the past. It might seem unlikely that an anorexic would develop binge eating disorder or vice versa but it's a surprisingly regular occurrence, because the way that sufferers respond to food is a symptom of the underlying mental health issues which most eating disorder sufferers have in common.

Alternative unhealthy coping mechanisms

Without food to turn to, some people who are recovering from an eating disorder will turn to self-harm and vice versa. For the same reason, students in recovery from self-harming and eating-disordered behaviours are at increased risk of substance or alcohol abuse, risky sexual activities and other unhealthy coping mechanisms. This is why it is so important for a student to explore a range of alternative methods for coping with their difficulties in a healthy, rather than harmful, way.

You can help to support a student through any of these eventualities as long as you are aware of them. So provide plenty of opportunities for the student to share their concerns with a trusted adult, and ensure that their friends remain vigilant.

How to support during relapses and rough patches

If it looks like things are taking a turn for the worse, address matters head on as quickly as possible, whilst remaining sensitive and supportive. The key thing to remember is that the student must not be made to feel that they've failed. More than likely they'll be beating themselves up and be feeling deeply upset that they're letting everyone around them down. This is a heavy burden to bear and you should aim not to exacerbate it by encouraging feelings of guilt. Instead, help the student to realize that this is simply a setback and nothing more…a detour rather than the end of the line.

Explore what has triggered the current difficulties
It won't always be possible to isolate the source of a setback but in many instances it may be that a particular incident has caused a setback, perhaps something someone has said or done. It is entirely likely that the offending action or comment was not intended to cause any offence or upset – sometimes even comments which are meant as compliments or to boost confidence can be misinterpreted and can trigger a setback. For instance the student recovering from an eating disorder who is told they are 'looking well', may interpret this to mean they're 'looking fat'. The student needs to feel able to share any difficulties such as this in confidence so similar situations can be avoided moving forward.

Offer more support if necessary
During a difficult period it may be necessary to increase the amount of support you offer to the student for a while. Discuss this option with them and let them guide you. Make sure that they feel able to ask for additional support at any time – this way they may be able to avoid a relapse situation by asking for extra support before things go too far.

Call for back-up
Don't feel you have to go it alone. If you feel it's appropriate, bring in the support of external agencies such as your local CAMHS, even if you had previously felt this was no longer necessary. Some schools want to show that they can manage things well internally, but making effective use of external agencies is a sign of strength and may ultimately be in the student's best interests. The waiting lists for such help can be long, so consider asking for help sooner rather than later. If you wait until you can't manage without extra support then you could end up in a difficult situation.

What does recovery look like?

The number one priority is a healthy, happy student. It's unrealistic to expect that the student will never again suffer any difficulties with food or self-harm. A big part of success is about the student becoming sufficiently self-aware to spot potential problems in their thoughts and behaviour in time to prevent a major relapse in the future.

Successfully beating self-harm or an eating disorder may involve making compromises such as:

- deferring exams
- performing less than perfectly in exams
- moving down a school year
- withdrawing from high-level competitions in a favourite sport or activity
- participating in fewer extracurricular activities.

These compromises may be seen as failures by the student, but they're not. If they are happy and choosing to eat healthily each day or are no longer using self-harm to cope, then they are succeeding and should be proud.

Success stories – students' point of view

'It was the hardest thing I ever had to do, but I did it. I haven't made myself sick for three years now. I have a steady job and a steady boyfriend, life is good!'

'Sometimes I still want to cut. But I don't. I have the strength to say "No, I don't need to." Every time that happens I feel so proud I could sing!'

'It's only now that I realize I could have actually died. I could literally have starved myself to death. At the time I probably wouldn't have cared but now I'm happy to be alive every day.'

'You don't realize how dark the dark times are until the bright times come along. Self-harm had taken over my life, but I feel like I'm actually in control now and good things are starting to happen.'

'For me, success is no longer about having a string of A*s and the perfect body, it's about being alive, doing my best and learning to love myself. I'm not so bad…'

Success stories – staff members' point of view

'There were a lot of ups and even more downs, but we got there in the end. It was a real team effort involving friends, parents and staff at school. He's finished school now but he comes back to say hi, and let us know that he's doing okay. I think we became quite special to him, as he did to us.'

'I felt completely out of my depth when she first confided in me, but I'm so glad she trusted me to help. She'll soon be sitting her GCSEs, a year later than planned. Her predicted grades are good – but, more importantly, she seems genuinely happy.'

'I had no idea how hard it would be to beat an eating disorder. She fought so hard and we were like her little army, behind her every step of the way. Life is beginning to return to normal for her now, which is just wonderful to see.'

'We had not seen him for years, then one day he came into school with his wife and his baby daughter. He told us about his job and his friends and how much he had come to love life. He turned to his wife and said – "This is Mrs Lyle, you know, the one I told you about who helped me want to live." She flung herself into my arms and whispered "Thank you".'

LEARNING TO TAKE AWAY FROM THIS CHAPTER

- Learning to overcome short-term setbacks is an important part of the long-term recovery process for students overcoming self-harm and eating disorders.
- Recovery can take many different forms and may involve compromises.

THINGS TO DO

- Celebrate stories of recovery and success amongst your past and current students. Take a moment to appreciate the journeys you and your students have been on and remember their happy endings when you go through more difficult times with other students in future.

Index

absenteeism 82
abuse 33, 58, 60, 69, 71–2
    physical harm 79
    reporting 108, 113, 128
    sexual abuse 58, 59
academic expectations 68, 70
    return to school 139–40, 144–5
achievement standards 68
addiction 35, 105
adolescents 26, 207–8
    adolescent behaviour 39
    personality change 81
    working with students post-
        16 108
advice, seeking 46, 49
affirmations 209
age of onset 36, 38, 42–3
age-appropriate teaching 42–3
agencies 133–4, 136–8
alcohol abuse 26, 36, 37, 69, 76,
    80, 207
Alexander, June *A Boy Called Tim* 38
alternatives to unhealthy behaviours
    198
    delaying tactics to give you a short
        time to think 201
    ideas for the middle of the night
        203
    ideas for when you feel alone or
        down 200
    ideas for when you need a
        distraction 201–2
    ideas for when you need to vent
        your feelings 199
    ideas for when you're confused
        202–3
    ideas that help you to understand
        and celebrate yourself
        205–6
    ideas that remind you that you
        have a future 205
    ideas that remind you that you're
        real 204–5
    ideas that simulate self-harm 198
    ideas that won't be noticed in
        busy situations 203–4
    ideas to help you feel more in
        control 200
    see also behavioural change
ambivalence 212
anniversaries 75–6
anonymity 46, 48
    anonymous helplines 44, 51,
        92–3, 101
    question boxes 49, 50
anorexia nervosa 18–19, 35
    blind people 33
    case studies 56–7, 172, 176,
        179–80

death rate 37
male patients 38
over-exercise and anorexia nervosa
    162
restricted eating and food rules 82
weight change 79
anxiety 24, 68, 147, 166–7
art 197
    art therapy 25
    creating something expressive 197
    creating something to destroy 198
    enabling expression through the
        act of creation 197
asking questions 49, 93–4
attention-seeking behaviours 33–4, 53
    invented self-harm 62–4
    why seek attention? 54, 64

behavioural change 207–8
    affirmations 209
    amplifying ambivalence 212
    developing discrepancy 211
    expressing empathy 211
    open questions 208–9
    reflective listening 209–10
    rolling with resistance 212–13
    supporting self-efficacy 213
    see also alternatives to unhealthy
        behaviours
binge eating disorder 21–2, 33, 35
    misconceptions 34
    weight change 79
bolt holes 147–8
breathing techniques 169
bulimia nervosa 19–21, 33, 35
    misconceptions 36–7
    wearing scarves 80
    weight change 79
bullying 72, 75, 152, 172

CAMHS 15, 127, 134–5, 217
    developing a positive relationships
        with external agencies 133
    getting the child's doctor on
        board 132
    how the referral process works
        129–30
    how to increase the likelihood of
        a successful CAMHS referral
        130–2
    supporting a child whilst they are
        receiving external support
        133–4
    when is specialist support needed?
        127–9
checklist for teaching students 50–1,
    52
chewing gum 80–1

Child and Adolescent Mental Health
    Services *see* CAMHS
child and family assessment teams
    (CAFATs) 26
children 15
    age-appropriate teaching 42–3
    difficulty expressing feelings and
        emotions 67
    eating problems specific to under-
        11s 22–3, 29
    food avoidance emotional disorder
        24–5
    food phobia 24
    food refusal 23
    restrictive eating 23
    selective eating 24
    third person 192
clothing, baggy or long 79–80
Common Assessment Framework
    (CAF) 133
communication skills 42
compliance 67–8
confidentiality 39, 93
    ground rules 45–6
    honesty 100–1
    maintaining trust without
        promising confidentiality
        105–8
confrontation 87
contact details 116
    providing CAMHS with contact
        details 131
control issues 56, 70, 108, 200
    anorexia nervosa 56–7
coping mechanisms 42, 53, 55–6
    alternatives to unhealthy
        behaviours 198–206
    control 56–7
    exposure to unhealthy coping
        mechanisms 75
    managing overwhelming feelings
        59–60
    nowhere else to turn 61
    punishment 58
    response to trauma 58–9, 70
    school holidays 167
    self-harm 36, 38
    wishing to feel cared for 61–2
    wishing to feel pure or clean 61
counselling 125, 148–9, 181, 195,
    207
cultural identity conflict 70–1
curriculum 41, 43, 44, 52, 146
cutting 60–1

dehydration 81
depression 24, 25, 37, 68, 82, 166–7
diabetes 26

disclosure 44, 45, 49, 50, 51, 52, 98, 112
  acknowledge how hard disclosure was 110
  agree next steps 111
  be honest 100
  confidentiality 100–1
  don't judge 99
  give the student information or helplines 111
  how difficult you find the situation 101–3
  how rapidly you can help 101
  how to respond if a student shows you their injuries 103–5
  ideas for encouraging reluctant talkers to open up 91–6
  listen 99
  maintaining trust without promising confidentiality 105–8
  make a record 111–12
  make time for student 98–9
  overcoming objections to informing parents 109–10
  persevere 99–100
  positive communication 87–91
  summarize what student has said 110–11
  what next? 110–12
discrepancy 211
discussing disorders 30, 40
  asking questions 49, 93–4
  avoiding making assumptions 48
  be practical 102–3
  be prepared for setbacks 103
  discussing disorders with students 41–2
  distancing the learning 47, 51
  encouraging openness 46
  encouraging seeking help and advice 49
  ensuring the right to pass 47–8
  ground rules 45–6, 50, 52
  increasing staff confidence in talking about sensitive issues 31–2
  keeping the conversation in the room 47
  listening to others 48
  maintaining a non-judgemental approach 47, 99
  potential learning outcomes 44
  remember the real child 102
  running parent workshops and information sessions 39–40
  take a child-centred approach 102
  try to understand 101–2
  using language carefully 48
dizziness 81
drug abuse 26, 69, 76, 80, 207

eating disorders 17–18, 29, 30, 207, 215
  age of onset 36, 38
  anorexia nervosa 18–19
  binge eating disorder 21–2
  bulimia nervosa 19–21
  common misconceptions 32–8, 40, 55
  concerns about appearance 33
  eating problems specific to under-11s 22–5

OSFED (Other Specified Feeding or Eating Disorder) 22
  poor hair, skin and nails 81
  scheduling activities during lunch 82
  toothache and headaches 81
  what you should teach 43
  why do students develop eating disorders? 55–62
  wishing to appear ugly 58–9
eating disorders recovery 159
  ideas to help at mealtimes 160–2
  safe participation in school sports 162–4
  what not to say 164–5
EDNOS (Eating Disorder Not Otherwise Specified) 22
educational psychologists 125
emotional wellbeing 30, 32, 40
  labelling 102
  neglect or any form of abuse 71–2
emotions 59–60
  developing new ways to express emotions 196–8
  difficulty expressing feelings and emotions 67
empathy 211
exam pressure 76
exercise 162–3
  exercise and sport as a means of relieving stress 164
  exercise diaries 163
external agencies 133–4
  working with external agencies 136–8

failure 19, 68, 73
  academic expectations 139, 146
  response to failure 145–6
fainting 81
family life 69
  children in care 71
  controlling or protective family 70
  cultural identity conflict 70–1
  family relationship difficulties 74–5
  illness in the family 76
  neglect or any form of abuse 71–2
  poor relationships with parents 72
  unreasonably high academic expectations 70
  young carer's role 71, 76
feelings 59–60
  alternatives to unhealthy behaviours 198–206
  difficulty expressing feelings and emotions 67
first aid 105
food rules 82
free passes 146–7
friends 40, 41, 172
  benefits of students being friends with other students who self-harm 158
  contact with friends during inpatient care 137–8
  dangers of students being friends with other students who self-harm 159
  friends who have suffered from self-harm or eating disorders 72–3

getting information from friends 85–6
  isolation 79
  peer relationship break up/difficulties 75
  peer support 141–2
  preparing staff and peers for student's return to school 142–3
  teaching students to support friends 45, 49

gender 72
group self-harm 151, 156–8

hair 81
headaches 81
help, seeking 42, 49
helplines 111
  anonymous helplines 44, 51, 92–3, 101
hobbies 73
honesty 100

impulsivity 69
information 111, 117
information sessions 39–40
injuries
  risks of exposing injuries and scars 151–2
  risks of not exposing injuries and scars 152–3
  should self-harm injuries and scars be covered? 151
  wound management and infection prevention 155–6
injuries, being shown 103
  acknowledge how hard this must have been 103
  don't ask what happened 103–4
  don't comment on the seriousness of their injuries 104
  don't expect them to understand why they did it 104
  don't make superficial comments 105
  don't over-react or trivialise 104
  don't tell them to stop 105
  first aid 105
inpatient care 136–7, 143
  contact with friends 137–8
  don't be afraid to ask for updates 137
  maintaining contact with inpatient unit during recovery 138
  maintaining contact with the unit during recovery 138
  providing academic work 137
  questions to ask the inpatient unit prior to student's return to school 142
  reintegrating students into school following inpatient treatment 138–43
internet 171–2, 182
  case studies 175–6, 179–80
  discouraging the use of pro-sites 177–8, 180–1
  list of eating disorders and self-harm slang terms commonly used online 173–4
  pro-ana, pro-mia and pro-harm sites 174

internet *cont.*
  safely educating students about
    pro-sites 179
  what to do if you're concerned
    179–81
  who uses pro-sites? 174–5
  why are pro-sites dangerous? 175
  why are pro-sites dangerous? 175
isolation 79

journalling 196–7

labelling 102
lateness 82
lifestyle choices 35, 174, 175, 177–8,
  182
listening to students 87–8, 99
  appropriate body language 89–90
  avoid time pressure 88, 98–9
  encouraging reluctant talkers 91–6
  keep your talking to a minimum
    90–1
  prove that you're listening 90
  reflective listening 209–10
  remove distractions 88–9
  seating arrangements 89
  use silence 93
lists 192
  choose a specific person 193
  length of lists 192
  location 193
  ten things that make me angry
    193–4
  ten things that make me feel calm
    194–5
  three people I can talk to when
    I'm in need of support
    195–6
  timeframe 192

mealtimes for recovering students 160
  after lunch matters too 162
  don't 'watch' 161
  don't discuss food and weight
    concerns over lunch 162
  don't talk about how much
    they've eaten 161
  let students eat with a friend or
    parent 160
  let students serve themselves 161
  meal timings and locations 160
  provide specific meals 161
  trust students to keep food diaries
    160
meeting parents 114
  agree next steps 116
  consider room set-up 115
  consider who should attend
    114–15
  focus on practical steps 116
  give them information to take
    away 117
  make sure you have tea and
    tissues 115
  remain objective 115–16
  share your contact details and be
    available 116
  think about location 114
mental health 30, 32, 40
  exam pressure 76
  labelling 102
  neglect or any form of abuse 71–2
  openness 46

personality change 81
running parent workshops and
  information sessions 39–40
misconceptions 32, 50, 64, 65
  eating disorders are a lifestyle
    choice 35
  eating disorders are a teenage
    phase 36, 55
  eating disorders aren't life
    threatening 37
  eating disorders stem from vanity
    and the media 33, 55
  it's easy to stop self-harming 35–6
  people who binge eat should eat
    less and exercise or more 34
  people who self-harm are crazy 36
  people who self-harm are suicidal
    34–5, 53
  people who self-harm don't feel
    pain 37
  purging is an effective way to lose
    weight 36–7
  self-harm and eating disorders are
    attention-seeking behaviours
    33–4, 53–4
  self-harm and eating disorders
    only affect girls 38–9
  you can't recover from an eating
    disorder 37–8
motivational interviewing 207–8, 214
  applying motivational
    interviewing at school
    213–14
  principles of motivational
    interviewing 210–13
  spirit of motivational interviewing
    208–10
multi-agency forums (MAFs 133

nails 81
National Collaborating Centre for
  Mental Health 28
neglect 60, 61, 69, 71–2
  reporting 108, 113, 128
non-judgemental approach 47, 99

objectivity 115–16
one-to-one support 183–4
  creating an environment for
    talking 186–7
  developing a recovery action plan
    187–9
  helping students feel comfortable
    enough to talk 189–96
  looking after staff wellbeing 186
  role of the school 184–6
open questions 208–9
openness 46
  keeping the conversation in the
    room 47
OSFED (Other Specified Feeding or
  Eating Disorder) 22

pain 37, 60
  cutting 60–1
panic attacks 146–8, 167
  afterwards, identify the trigger
    169
  assert control 168
  don't be afraid to talk about it
    169–70
  don't make assumptions or be
    dismissive 168

don't panic 168
focus on breathing 169
give the sufferer space and time
  169
just be there 167
move away from the cause 168
parents 15, 106, 108, 109, 113–14,
  126
  consent to strategies for
    minimizing harm 155
  dealing with difficult scenarios
    119–23
  first meeting 114–17
  I don't want to worry them 109
  informing via telephone 117–19
  parents who don't think the
    school should be involved
    122–3
  parents who think you're blaming
    them for their child's
    difficulties 120–1
  parents who think you're blowing
    up the problem out of
    proportion 121–2
  poor relationships with parents 72
  running parent workshops and
    information sessions 39–40
  supporting other people's children
    39–40
  supporting recovery 123–5
  they won't understand 109
  they'll be angry 109–10
perfectionism 58, 68
perseverance 86–7
  create opportunities for students to
    speak to you 86–7
personality change 81
personality factors 66–7
  compliance 67–8
  difficulty expressing feelings and
    emotions 67
  impulsivity or drug and alcohol
    use 69
  low mood, anxiety and low self-
    esteem 68–9
  poor problem-solving skills 69
  very high expectations of
    achievement 68
physical education avoidance 80
physical harm 79
play dough 186, 190
  interpreting image of self 191–2
  make a face 191
  model scenarios 190
  relieving anger 190
  size of ball 191
  third person 192
  use colours to represent mood 191
  used as distraction 190
play therapy 25
poetry 197
police 76
policies 31–2, 40, 113
  safeguarding policies 46, 47, 49,
    122, 135, 136
private healthcare 129
problem-solving skills 42, 69
procedures 31–2, 40
psychiatry 136, 181
punishment issues 58
purging 36–7

question boxes 49, 50–1

rape 33, 58, 59, 128
record keeping 111–12, 219
recovery 37–8, 215, 219
    blips during eating disorder
        recovery 215–16
    child-centred approach 102–3
    key pointers for helping the
        student feel in control 124
    maintaining contact with inpatient
        unit during recovery 138
    person-centred approach 123–4
    recovery goals 125
    recovery teams 123, 124–5
    reintegrating students into
        school following inpatient
        treatment 138–43
    setbacks 103
    setting goals 124–5
    success stories 218–19
    support during relapses and rough
        patches 216–17
    what does recovery look like?
        217–18
    see school holidays and recovering
        students; supporting
        recovery at school
recovery action plans 187
    feedback loop 189
    how will you measure success and
        track progress? 188
    what can you do? 188–9
    what is your aim? 188
referrals 129–30
    demonstrate day-to-day impact of
        the child's difficulties 131–2
    ensure that a referral is needed
        130
    outline ways in which the school
        has already tried to help
        132
    providing CAMHS with contact
        details 131
    situations where a student should
        always be referred 128–9,
        185
    write a full and thorough referral
        130–1
relapses 145, 215–216
    back-up for school staff 217
    developing different forms of
        eating and self-harm
        disorders 216
    relapse warning signs 141
    support during relapses and rough
        patches 216–17
religious fasting 61
resilience factors 73–4
resistance to change 212–13
responsibility 31, 40
restricted eating 82
return to school 138
    academic expectations 139–40,
        144–5
    identifying triggers 140–1
    peer support 141–2
    phased return to school 138–9
    preparing staff and peers for
        student's return to school
        142–3
    questions to ask the inpatient unit
        prior to student's return to
        school 142

understanding relapse warning
    signs 141
risk factors 66, 77
    family life 69–72
    personality 66–9
    resilience 73–4, 77
    social life 72–3
    triggers 74–6, 77

safe places, designated 147–8
safeguarding 26, 31, 41, 49
school policies 46, 47, 49, 122,
    135, 136
scars 151–3
school holidays and recovering
    students 165
    consider who students can turn to
        for help at home 166
    discuss how students feel about
        holidays 165–6
    discuss who is currently aware of
        students' difficulties 166
    explore healthy coping
        mechanisms 166–7
    think about what other sources of
        support are available 166
    think about what students' typical
        day will look like 166–7
school staff 30, 40
    discussing mental health and
        emotional wellbeing
        concerns 32
    discussing sensitive issues 31–2,
        51, 52
    looking after staff wellbeing 186
    one-to-one support 183–4
    policies and procedures 31–2
    preparing staff and peers for
        student's return to school
        142–3
    proactive support to sufferers 31
    regular access to a trusted adult
        148–9
    role of the school 184–6
    running parent workshops and
        information sessions 39–40
    talking to other members of staff
        84–5
    training 31
secretive behaviour 54, 106
    baggy or long clothing 79–80
self-efficacy 213
self-esteem 19, 21, 22, 25, 33, 34,
    68–9, 82, 152
self-harm 25, 29, 30, 215
    adapting self-harm behaviours to
        make them less dangerous
        154–5
    alternative coping mechanism
        36, 38
    attention-seeking behaviour 33–4
    boys 38
    case studies 60–1, 62–3, 172,
        175–6
    common forms of self-harm 26
    common misconceptions 32–8,
        40, 53–4
    difficulty stopping 35–6
    how to respond if a student shows
        you their injuries 103–5
    indirect self-harm 26
    pain 37

responding to invented or
    imagined self-harm 62–4
responding to self-harm fads and
    group self-harm 151, 156–8
secretive behaviour 54
self-harm and suicide 28, 34–5,
    54
severity of behaviours 27
signs of shock 155
suicide risk 34–5
terms used to describe self-
    harm 27
what you should teach 43
why do students develop self-harm
    disorders? 55–62
wishing to appear ugly 58–9
wishing to feel cared for 61–2
wound management and infection
    prevention 155–6
self-harm recovery 150–1
    benefits of students being friends
        with other students who
        self-harm 158
    compromise 153
    dangers of students being friends
        with other students who
        self-harm 159
    ground rules for groups 158
    minimizing harm when the child
        is not ready to stop 153–4
    providing thinking time or
        alternatives to self-harm 154
    risks of exposing injuries and scars
        151–2
    risks of not exposing injuries and
        scars 152–3
    should self-harm injuries and scars
        be covered? 151
sexuality 72
shock 155
skin 81
social life 72
    being bullied or teased 72
    confusion about sexuality or
        gender 72
    friends who have suffered from
        self-harm or eating disorders
        72–3
    going out more or less 80
    highly competitive hobbies 73
special needs 25, 26, 69
specialist support 127–8
    choosing a private provider of
        specialist healthcare 129
    developing a positive relationship
        with external agencies 133
    getting the child's doctor on
        board 132
    increasing the likelihood of a
        successful CAMHS referral
        130–2
    referral process 129–30
    situations where a student should
        always be referred 128–9,
        185
    supporting a child whilst they are
        receiving external support
        133–4
sport avoidance 80
sports participation 162
    determine which types of activities
        are most acceptable 164

sports participation *cont.*
ensure weight/physique is not a
focal point for coaches 164
exercise and sport as a means of
relieving stress 164
exercise diaries 163
over-exercise and anorexia nervosa
162
seek guidance from health
providers 163
social aspect of school sport 162
work with parents 163
work with the student to agree a
healthy exercise plan 163
storytelling 197
stress 71, 72, 73
exercise and sport as a means of
relieving stress 164
trouble in school or with the
police 76
stress management 42
students 15
discussing disorders 45–9
participation in discussing
disorders 47–8
teaching students about eating
disorders and self-harm
41–5
suicide 28, 29, 34–5, 37, 128
supporting recovery at school 144,
170, 206
academic expectations 144–5
alternatives to unhealthy
behaviours 198–206
being helpful in class 150
considering the curriculum 146
developing new ways to express
emotions 196–8
free pass and bolt hole 146–8
how to support a student who
is having a panic attack
167–70
preparing for holidays 165–7
regular access to a trusted adult
148–9
response to failure 145–6
specific strategies for working
with students suffering from
eating disorders 159–65
specific strategies for working
with students who self-harm
150–9
using lists to support students in
recovery 192–6
supporting sufferers 31, 40
child-centred approach 102
don't wait too long 86
family relationship difficulties
74–5
locating sources of school, local
and national support 51, 52
teaching students to support
friends 45
see specialist support
symptoms 78, 83
early warning signs to look out
for 78–82
importance of spotting signs
early 78

talking to students 84, 96–7
ask open questions 93–4
create opportunities for them to
speak to you 86–7

creating an environment for
talking 186–7
do an activity 95
don't be confrontational 87
don't wait too long 86
encouraging reluctant talkers 91–6
explore things through the third
person 94–5
get information from their friends
85–6
helping students feel comfortable
enough to talk 189–96
positive communication 87–91
reassure them 92
remind them why they're here
95–6
start with small talk 93
talk about what will happen next
92–3
talk to other members of staff
84–5
use silence 93
when should you say something?
84–7
you might not be the best person
for the job 96
tea 110, 115
teaching students about disorders
41–2, 52
age-appropriate teaching 42–3
checklist 50–1, 52
consider vulnerable students 50
distancing the learning 47, 51
ending the lesson 52
familiarize yourself with school
policies 50
give the pupils the chance to
submit questions 50–1
locating sources of school, local
and national support 51, 52
potential learning outcomes 44
promoting discussion 45–9
reviewing lesson content 51
teaching students to support
friends 45
telling relevant staff you'll be
covering this topic 51
what you should teach 43
teasing 72
telephoning parents 117
ask for their support 119
ask how they feel about things
119
call at a good time 118
checklist 118
choose the most appropriate
parents 117 117
encourage questions 119
focus on the call 118
get to the point 119
plan what to say 117
suggest a face-to-face meeting 119
telling other people about disclosures
105–6
allowing the student to feel in
control 108
how will you tell them? 107
involving the student 106
overcoming objections to
informing parents 109–10
what will you say? 107
when not to tell 108
who should you talk to? 106

why should you talk to them?
106–7
working with students post-
16 108
tissues 110, 115
toilet trips 79
toothache 81
training 15
school staff 31
transition to a new school 76
trauma 24, 34, 38, 70, 71, 75, 128
anniversaries 75–6
response to sexual abuse 58–9
treatment 133–4
triggers 74
being exposed to unhealthy
coping mechanisms 75
bullying 75
difficult times of year 75–6
exam pressure 76
family relationship difficulties
74–5
identifying triggers 140–1
illness in the family 76
panic attacks 169
peer relationship break up/
difficulties 75
relapses 217
transition to a new school 76
trauma 75
trouble in school or with the
police 76

understanding 102–3

warning signs 78, 83
absence and lateness 82
baggy or long clothing 79–80
chewing gum or drinking water
80–1
dizziness 81
going out more or less 80
isolation 79
personality change 81
physical education/sport
avoidance 80
physical harm 79
poor hair, skin and nails 81
restricted eating and food rules 82
scheduling activities during
lunch 82
toilet trips 79
toothache and headaches 81
understanding relapse warning
signs 141
weight change 79
water 80–1
websites 15
pro-sites 174–81
weight change 79
baggy or long clothing 79–80
weight loss 36–7
what not to say to recovering students
164–5
avoid commenting on the
student's appearance 164–5
consider lesson content 165
don't define the student by their
eating disorder 165
workshops 39–40
wound management 155–6
writing 196–7

young carers 71, 76